PRAISE FOR
NOT A DAY CARE

"You must read this book. Everett Piper is a man of courage and conviction. He stands nearly alone as an academic leader confronting the ideological fascism of the snowflake rebellion. His call for intellectual freedom must be heard."

—GLENN BECK

"While others run from the battle Piper shows over and over again at least one person is willing to run toward it...Finally, a voice of sanity in the halls of the ivory tower..."

—JOSH McDOWELL, author and speaker

"Dr. Piper represents a voice of reason amidst the insanity and pabulum of the current generation!"

—STEVE LARGENT, member of the NFL Hall of Fame and former Oklahoma congressman

"Finally, some clarity in our murky times! Everett Piper exposes the shallowness and tragedy of so much of modern education."

—SEAN McDOWELL, author and speaker

"The tallest trees take the wind. Everett Piper is a redwood. To grow tall, each tree needs air, water, sun, and nutrients. For us to grow tall, we need the vitals of a tree and much more: learning, morals, ideals, courage, humility, and a stretch for excellence. Piper shows us how to stretch and to get there. It is a must read."

—FRANK KEATING, former governor of Oklahoma

"Snowflakes will melt when confronted by the global economic war already underway. The world doesn't offer 'safe spaces.' Fortunately, Dr. Everett Piper is training critical thinkers ready to lead America. His candle of truth in the darkness can and must redirect the course of higher education back to the path of sanity."

—KEVIN D. FREEMAN, *New York Times* bestselling author and host of *Economic War Room*

"Despite the blizzards of insanity generated by our 'learning' institutions, Dr. Piper stands guard over the warming fire of truth."

—SAM SORBO, actress and author of *They're YOUR Kids* and *Teach from Love*

"Dr. Piper is a dose of reality in a world of college fantasies. He says and does whatever college presidents ought to say, but won't."

—**JIM GARLOW**, pastor, speaker, and *New York Times* bestselling author of *Cracking da Vinci's Code*

"Dr. Piper is one of the leading thinkers in America. Everyone should read this book."

—**KELLY SHACKELFORD**, Esq., president, CEO, and Chief Counsel, First Liberty Institute

"It seems that while nearly all other college presidents cower in the face of today's student protests, Dr. Everett Piper is the only one to step forward with confidence and courage…"

—**KEVIN SORBO**, actor, speaker, and writer

"'Rugged American individualism' … 'The Puritan work ethic' …'The Greatest Generation'…Such are the phrases that made America the greatest nation in the world. Now we are talking 'snowflakes,' 'safe spaces,' and 'trigger alerts'? Not Piper. He challenges the rising generation to get some backbone, pick up the mantle, and retake lost ground."

—**DAVID BARTON**, author and founder of Wall Builders Radio

"There are very few in the ranks of academia with the courage to confront the nonsense of 'snowflakes' and their 'safe spaces' and Dr. Piper leads this small band of courageous souls."

—**TONY PERKINS**, president, Family Research Council

"Dr. Piper continues to protect civil discourse, one of the hallmarks of education. With his example, there is hope that the university is not a lost cause."

—**BOB McEWEN**, executive director, Council for National Policy

"My friend Everett Piper has a way of getting to the heart of issues quickly with very few words, and then leaves you with wisdom, sound advice, and great knowledge."

—**ALAN R. OSMOND**, Osmond Brothers, One Heart Foundation

NOT A DAY CARE

DR. EVERETT PIPER

PRESIDENT, OKLAHOMA WESLEYAN UNIVERSITY

WITH **BILL BLANKSCHAEN**

NOT A DAY CARE

THE DEVASTATING CONSEQUENCES OF ABANDONING TRUTH

REGNERY
FAITH

Regnery Faith™ is a trademark of Salem Communications Holding Corporation; Regnery® is a registered trademark of Salem Communications Holding Corporation

Scriptures taken from the Holy Bible, New International Version®, NIV®. Copyright © 1973, 1978, 1984, 2011 by Biblica, Inc.™ Used by permission of Zondervan. All rights reserved worldwide. www.zondervan.com The "NIV" and "New International Version" are trademarks registered in the United States Patent and Trademark Office by Biblica, Inc.™

Cataloging-in-Publication data on file with the Library of Congress

First E-book edition 2017: ISBN 978-1-62157-612-9
Originally published in hardcover, 2017: ISBN 978-1-62157-605-1

Published in the United States by
Regnery Faith
An imprint of Regnery Publishing
A Division of Salem Media Group
300 New Jersey Ave NW
Washington, DC 20001
www.RegneryFaith.com

Manufactured in the United States of America

10 9 8 7 6 5 4 3 2 1

Books are available in quantity for promotional or premium use. For information on discounts and terms, please visit our website: www.Regnery.com.

Distributed to the trade by
Perseus Distribution
www.perseusdistribution.com

CONTENTS

1

CRYING OURSELVES TO DEATH

TRIGGER WARNING! If you are a university administrator, faculty member, or a millennial "snowflake" on most college campuses today, what you are about to read may alarm, disturb, and offend you:

> Love is patient, love is kind. It does not envy, it does not boast, it is not proud. It does not dishonor others, it is not self-seeking, it is not easily angered, it keeps no record of wrongs. Love does not delight in evil but rejoices with the truth. It always protects, always trusts, always hopes, always perseveres.

If you read that quintessential love passage from 1 Corinthians and failed to see a problem, you're not alone. I share your confusion. This story hearkens back to Thanksgiving week 2015. I was going about my daily business as president of Oklahoma Wesleyan University (OKWU) when one of my vice presidents called me: "Dr. Piper, I wanted to give you a heads up. One of our students confronted me after I spoke in the chapel service this morning. He told me I should have had a trigger warning prior to my sermon because it offended him and made him feel uncomfortable. He claimed I 'singled him out' and, likewise, his peers. They felt unsafe by my egregious micro-aggression. What I said in my homily 'victimized' him."

Bewildered, I asked to review the text of my vice president's sermon, knowing that he always spoke from prepared notes and seldom ventured from them. "By the way," I asked, "what was the topic of your talk?" His response blew me away: "It was a sermon from 1 Corinthians 13—on love!"

You've likely heard 1 Corinthians 13 read at numerous weddings, perhaps even your own. After receiving the sermon text, I carefully read it to be sure I wasn't missing something. I found no sarcasm and absolutely zero political content. There wasn't even an attempt at humor that might have been misconstrued as offensive or insensitive. It was a clear call to Christian charity, nothing more and nothing less.

Having worked in academia my entire career, very little that happens on college campuses surprises me. But I was simply amazed that I was being confronted with this absurdity at a private, conservative Christian university that still boldly and unapologetically celebrates an educational paradigm solidly grounded in a biblical worldview. No one visiting our campus could miss our distinctly Christian mission and message. We proudly boast of the primacy of Christ, the priority of Scripture, the pursuit of truth, and the practice of wisdom. Our university motto reads, "Impacting Culture with the Lordship of Jesus Christ." We require chapel attendance twice a week and hold our students accountable to honor traditional morality and live lives of integrity and personal chastity. We boldly state who we are to every prospective student and parent and are crystal clear about what is expected of all members of our community.

Nevertheless, we had a student complaining that a sermon on love made him feel uncomfortable for being *unloving*! I responded with an open letter posted on our university website. Here is what it said:

> This past week, I actually had a student come forward after a university chapel service and complain because he felt "victimized" by a sermon on the topic of 1 Corinthians 13. It appears this young scholar felt offended because a homily on love made him feel bad for not showing love. In his mind, the speaker was wrong for making him and his peers feel uncomfortable.
>
> I'm not making this up. Our culture has actually taught students to be this self-absorbed and narcissistic. Any time their feelings are hurt, they are the victims. Anyone who dares to challenge them and, thus, makes them "feel bad" about themselves, is a "hater," a "bigot," an "oppressor," and a "victimizer."
>
> Well, I have a message for this young man and all others who care to listen. That feeling of discomfort you have after listening to a sermon is called a conscience. An altar call is supposed to make you feel bad. It is supposed to make you feel guilty. The goal

of many a good sermon is to get you to confess your sins—not coddle you in your selfishness. The primary objective of the Church and the Christian faith is your confession, not your self-actualization.

So here's my advice: If you want the chaplain to tell you you're a victim rather than tell you that you need virtue, this may not be the university you're looking for. If you want to complain about a sermon that makes you feel less than loving for not showing love, this might be the wrong place.

If you're more interested in playing the "hater" card than you are in confessing your own hate; if you want to arrogantly lecture, rather than humbly learn; if you don't want to feel guilt in your soul when you are guilty of sin; if you want to be enabled rather than confronted, there are many universities across the land (in Missouri and elsewhere) that will give you exactly what you want, but Oklahoma Wesleyan isn't one of them.

At OKWU, we teach you to be selfless rather than self-centered. We are more interested in you practicing personal forgiveness than political revenge. We want you to model interpersonal reconciliation rather than foment personal conflict. We believe the content of your character is more important than the color of your skin. We don't believe that you have been victimized every time you feel guilty and we don't issue "trigger warnings" before altar calls.

Oklahoma Wesleyan is not a "safe place," but rather, a place to learn: to learn that life isn't about you, but about others; that the bad feeling you have while listening to a sermon is called guilt; that the way to address it is to repent of everything that's wrong with you rather than blame others for everything that's wrong with them. This is a place where you will quickly learn that you need to grow up. *This is not a day care. This is a university.*

"IT'S ABOUT TIME SOMEONE SAID IT!"

A week later, the post had gone viral, shared by millions of people around the world. It became known as the "This is Not a Day Care" post and was featured on The O'Reilly Factor, The Kelly File, FOX and Friends, Varney and Company, NBC Today, and dozens of other local and regional news outlets. *The American Spectator, The Federalist, The Washington Post,* and *The New York Times* all covered the story. *The Drudge Report,* blogger Rod Dreher, and syndicated radio host Dr. Drew picked it up. Rush Limbaugh and Glenn Beck praised the story. My willingness to state what seemed to me to be obvious had started a bit of a wildfire among people frustrated by the "snowflake rebellion" on college campuses across America and around the world. My phone rang off the hook as emails and letters poured in from parents, frustrated at paying tens of thousands of dollars to have their children brainwashed and bullied, saying, "Thank you! It's about time someone said it!"

I wrote that post a little over eighteen months ago, but the snowflake rebellion hasn't lessened. If anything, it has devolved into a blizzard of self-absorbed insanity. Microaggressions, trigger warnings, and demands for "safe spaces" continue to dominate campus news from coast to coast. Students at Emory University cried for counseling because someone used chalk to write the name of a presidential candidate on a campus sidewalk. Yale professors were forced to resign because several young scholars didn't like their views about Halloween costumes.

At American University, the University of Wyoming, and UC San Diego, students receive coloring books to help alleviate stress and cope with anxiety. Not to be outdone, Brown University created a "safe space" for students that included "cookies, coloring books, bubbles, Play-Doh, calming music, pillows, blankets, and a video of puppies." And Southern Illinois University just announced its brilliant plan to host coordinated campus "naps" where its students can snuggle up together in sleeping bags at the university's library and "dream of diversity" as they seek to solve the nation's ills.

The election results in 2016 sent thousands of students at campuses across the country into whining fits of rage with #notmypresident flooding social media. At Pitt, students blocked streets and destroyed public property while chanting, "Our streets! Our streets!" Meanwhile, they formed a "healing circle" for potentially offended students—offended not by the student protests and riots, of course, but by the results of the election—at the university library.[1] Several teachers cancelled classes or postponed exams to help students cope with what they called "a life-changing event" and "one of the most shocking events in our history."[2]

Who can forget the social media images of student protesters screaming in anguish as President Trump took the oath of office? One professor told her class that the election of Trump was "an act of terrorism."[3] The same professor suggested those who committed the assault were "amongst us" and required students who voted for Trump to stand. A student at Berkeley was attacked and beaten for daring to wear a "Make America Great Again" hat.[4]

Meanwhile as they encourage students to ignore political realities, learned leaders of campuses across the country have forsaken science as well, insisting there is no biological or physiological distinction between males and females. As the result, nothing less than total "gender" chaos has ensued. A Canadian professor faces criminal charges for refusing to use a new set of pronouns to describe fictitious "gender" categories. In New Zealand, a young man, who now "identifies" as a woman, is setting weight lifting records by competing in the women's division. A transgender athlete from Hawaii appears to be on his way to the Olympics after declaring himself to be a woman and switching to the woman's division of USA Volleyball. At the University of Kansas, students were offered buttons to announce their preferred pronouns. Champlain College took it one step further, offering this version so as not to offend: "Hello, my pronouns are fluid. Please ask me!"

Biological facts have been flushed down the toilet, as college bathrooms have become laboratories for social experimentation and university classrooms have become platforms for ideological indoctrination and, as the result, women suffer the loss of their facilities, their sports, their privacy and their very identity. And all who dare to speak of the reality of the twenty-third chromosomal pair and suggest that women are real, and not merely the contrived fantasies of subjective social constructs, are harassed into silence.

No longer are college campuses bulwarks of free thought and speech—in fact, they haven't been for a long time. The same Woodstock-attending flower children of the 1960s who called for love and understanding—and then stormed campus offices and indulged in sit-ins and riots—now teach students to silence mostly conservative dissenters through disruptive violence.

Rioters at Berkeley threw a violent tantrum, hurling explosives at police officers, when a purported conservative speaker dared to arrive on campus.[5] University of Missouri professor Melissa Click infamously called for "muscle" to remove a student journalist who was trying to report on a campus protest. Student leadership at Santa Clara University rejected a conservative club because it might make some students feel "uncomfortable."[6]

A professor at the University of Northern Colorado was shut down for asking students to examine varying viewpoints on such controversial issues as transgenderism, gay marriage, abortion, and global warming. After complaints that some students felt uncomfortable, the professor was warned to stay away from discussing alternative views on such topics. One student actually complained that, "students are required to watch the in-class debate and hear both arguments presented."[7]

The stories seem endless. Millennials feel uncomfortable. They demand to be coddled. And spineless college administrators and their shamelessly complicit faculty readily comply.

It may be tempting to dismiss what's happening on university campuses as disconnected from the "real world" where most people live. But what happens in the classroom doesn't stay on the campus. Whether it is the bullying dismissal of other points of view or the gender nonsense that has become ideological orthodoxy on college campuses, we should expect to see more of it on Main Street. For example, anti-Trump leftist protesters, acting in a way familiar to any college administrator, disrupted a chaplain trying to pray and verbally abused a Vietnam War vet at a Louisiana town hall meeting trying to lead the pledge of allegiance.[8] In New York City, businesses can now be fined up to $250,000 for refusing to address someone by a preferred pronoun—and there are thirty-one possible "gender" categories.[9]

And is it any wonder that students have so little respect for the law of the land when so many colleges and universities have declared their schools to be sanctuary campuses in violation of federal law, even as they readily accept massive amounts of federal funding?

Today's law students are tomorrow's lawyers and judges— and if you wonder why so many judges legislate from the bench, take a look at what they teach in law school. Today's business students are tomorrow's business leaders—and if you wonder why so many corporations are so politically correct, take a look at what they teach at business school. The students who want to ban Plato, Aristotle, Voltaire, and Kant from college curricula will soon be sitting on school boards or serving in academia. The students who believe in shutting down unpopular and often conservative points of view will soon be leading our state legislatures.[10] What is taught in the classroom today will be practiced in the real world tomorrow.

God help us. If we do not halt this slide into absurdity, our coddled campuses will produce a crippled America. As a university president, I care deeply about the state of American colleges and universities. I presently have the privilege of serving an academic community that proudly and explicitly acknowledges its Christian commitment and biblical heritage. I know the challenges faced on the secular campuses, as well. I've worked at five different universities, public and private, and earned my doctorate from Michigan State University. In addition, I have two college-aged sons, so I fully understand the parental side of the equation.

I know the financial pressures faced by university presidents, perhaps more than most. When I arrived at Oklahoma Wesleyan University a little more than a decade ago, the school was a year away from closing its doors. Our debt nearly matched our revenue, and we didn't have the luxury of a multi-billion-dollar endowment. We had to deliver real results in the real world.

I'm proud to say that we did just that. Today Oklahoma Wesleyan University is not only on sound financial footing, but our faculty is among the very best in the nation, ranked number one by students in national surveys. I couldn't be prouder of what our entire team has accomplished, and yet we still encounter the same nonsense about trigger warnings and safe spaces—even when spreading messages of love in chapel.

Because my interviews with Bill O'Reilly, Stuart Varney, Steve Doocy, and hundreds of other journalists have put me in the spotlight, I have been asked by college leaders and countless concerned parents across America, "How did we get here and what's the solution?" This book is my answer to that question. But we can start with a simple response.

As Richard Weaver reminded us seventy years ago in his book of the same name, "ideas have consequences." The ideas that dominate higher education are bankrupt and the consequences are dire. Universities are no longer interested in pursuing truth; indeed, they often deny that there is such a thing as truth. Instead, they celebrate tolerance, a very limited tolerance as it turns out, as they are intolerant of anyone who disagrees with them.

Today, college campuses are bastions of speech codes and ideological conformity. Faculty and students alike are more interested in identifying "trigger warnings" than they are in pursuing truth. For decades, our schools have taught that all morality is relative; they have promoted the "cultural Marxist" position that race, sex, and class are what matters; they have derided America, Western civilization, and Christianity as deeply flawed and deeply oppressive. We are now seeing the results of that teaching, not only on college campuses, but in our culture, in our laws, and in our political life. In the universities few are willing to speak out against these illiberal tendencies.

Former Stanford Provost John Etchemendy is an exception. In a 2017 speech to Stanford University's Board of Trustees, he said:

> Over the years, I have watched a growing intolerance at universities in this country…a kind of intellectual intolerance, a political one-sidedness, that is the antithesis of what universities should stand for…. This results in a kind of intellectual blindness that will, in the long run, be more damaging to universities…because we won't even see it: We will write off those with opposing views as evil or ignorant or stupid, rather than as interlocutors worthy of consideration. We succumb to the all-purpose *ad hominem* because it is easier and more comforting than rational argument. But when we do, we abandon what is great about this institution we serve.[11]

I'm sure Dr. Etchemendy and I would disagree on many things, but we would agree on this: the purpose of the university is the pursuit of truth. Yet truth is precisely what is most unwelcome at so many universities today that insist on protecting students from having to encounter it.

But there is an answer to this absurdity. It is found in the historical liberal arts and the premise that there are certain moral and intellectual laws tested by time, defended by reason, validated by experience, and endowed to us by our Creator that we can discover through free inquiry. Dozens of universities were once emblazoned with the motto, "You shall know the truth and the truth shall set you free." The University of California has the motto, *Fiat Lux*, "Let there be light." That is what a university should be about—about truth, about light—and today most universities aren't about that at all.

In the pages that follow, I reveal how bad the problem has become—even at schools deemed conservative or Christian in their heritage—and the harmful consequences our nation will suffer if we do not change, and change quickly. I'll explore the cultural implications of the slide into "snowflake" insanity, offer practical advice for parents, students, and concerned Americans, and empower you, I hope, to defend what you know to be true against the loud but vacuous cultural and academic Left that threatens to destroy both our universities and our country.

2

THE SNOWFLAKE INSANITY

I t's not enough that we coddle students on college campuses today. Students now want to be paid to be pacified. Resident assistants (RAs) at Scripps College, a prestigious school for women, posted signs earlier this year claiming students should be compensated for "emotional labor," which they defined as "the exertion of energy for the purpose of addressing people's feelings, educating, making people comfortable or living up to social 'expectations.'" We used to call this "playing nice with others," the price we all pay for participating in the human story. Now students want to be paid for developing basic people skills and the burden of interacting with others unlike themselves.

The RAs posted two signs, one on white paper and titled "Quick Guide for White Students" and one on black paper titled "Quick Guide For People Of Color And Marginalized

Backgrounds," a.k.a. everyone else. I shudder to ponder the reaction great leaders such as Martin Luther King Jr., Booker T. Washington, or Frederick Douglass would have to such blanket divisions of people based solely on the color of their skin. Yet the two signs made it quite clear that students at Scripps College were segregated by race and should think and act accordingly.

The sign for non-white students offered tips on how to know if they are "victims of emotional labor" and suggested action steps, including to refer people to Google to get educated, to bring in peers or professors to do the education, and to "charge for your services. If you've decided you're going to do it [engage], at least get paid for it." In what version of reality, I ask, does this approach make sense to anyone? How far we have come from Martin Luther King's dream that his "four little children would one day live in a nation where they would not be judged by the color of their skin, but by the content of their character"?

Conversely, the sign addressed to white students offered ways to know if they are causing emotional labor. (Note that it is assumed that only one group could be the victim of this manufactured offense, and the other group, by definition, was necessarily the offender and the victimizer.) The sign challenged white students to ask themselves these questions:

- Could I have Googled the answer but I chose not to?
- Do I find myself in a situation where people of color or people from a marginalized group are educating me?
- What power dynamics are at play?
- Do I find myself getting defensive?

- Are people telling me I'm causing them emotional labor?

The poster encouraged white students to hang out with other students who are educating themselves about "social justice issues" and to "pay for the labor they cause," and—wait for it— "do better next time!"[1]

Snowflake students at Oberlin College in May 2016 also demanded they be paid for protesting and engaging in activism—$8.20 per hour sounded about right to them. The students behind the creation of the petition whined that they were unable to keep up with coursework because late night political activism cut into their sleep. More than 1,300 students, on a campus with fewer than 3,000 students, signed the petition that included demands to discard any grade below a C. They also demanded less stressful alternatives to written midterm examinations, such as having conversations with professors instead of taking tests.[2]

On the one hand, students claimed Oberlin College needs to stop being an institution of "oppression" and get with the rest of the world in "incorporating everybody." At the same time, these students readily admit that "everybody" excludes anybody outside their narrowly defined category of victimization as determined by race, sex, gender identity, or class—all this at "a school whose norms may run a little to the left of Bernie Sanders," as a reporter for *The New Yorker* described it.[3]

Our universities are doing a tremendous disservice, both to students and our culture, by letting students think they can bend reality to fit their whims. In the real world, people don't get paid to be selfish and disruptive, but, rather, to be productive members of society. They are rewarded for cooperation and teamwork, not for dividing people because they have negative feelings about another race or feel offended by those from a different socioeconomic background. Our universities are producing a generation of Americans who are unable to function in the real world. We are quickly becoming a culture of Peter Pans, believing we can avoid reality in a Neverland of our own making. We're encouraging students to embrace their selfish fantasies and to expect everyone around them to bend and submit to their narcissistic whims and personal prejudices. We have created a generation that expects to receive affirmation for every feeling they have and every emotion they feel. Objective reality doesn't matter. Subjective opinions are king.

Many of today's universities seem content to give degrees in opinions, as opposed to degrees grounded in knowledge and the classical pursuit of wisdom, beauty, and truth. I once warned our graduating students of this danger in an Oklahoma Wesleyan commencement address:

> Today we are all here to celebrate! You have made it. This is your day. You have completed your last final exam and handed in your last paper and now it is your graduation day and you are here with your moms and dads and grandmothers and grandfathers to celebrate your commencement ceremonies here at OKWU. Congratulations!
>
> Over the next few minutes I'm going to give you a long-winded commencement address. (I should know better, for it surely isn't why you're here.) But after I'm done, I'm going to call you up to the stage. You'll stand to my left and wait for your name to be called. Then you'll march proudly across the stage. I'll, thereby, shake your hand, give you your diploma, and

whisper in your ear, "Congratulations! You now have a degree in opinions."

What I just said is absurd and you know it. After four years of studying, and four years of quizzes, and four years of tests, four years of paying tuition, four years of the rigor of the academy, all you have to show for it are opinions? That's insulting, isn't it? I surely hope you got more than that from your college education! Today, as you graduate, I do not care what your opinion is, nor should you care that much about mine. You did not major in opinions. I'm not going to give you a diploma in opinions. A good education is not about opinions. It's about learning what's true.

Pol Pot, Mao, Robespierre, Stalin, Chavez, Hitler, Mussolini and all the despots of history had opinions—and it did not end well. Opinions always lead to slavery and bondage, but Jesus told us that the truth shall set you free. I surely hope that if you majored in nursing that you have a little more knowledge today of the truths of biology, physiology, and chemistry than you did before you came here. Because if you're going to administer medication to me on the basis of your opinion, stay away from me. You are dangerous. If you're going to design an airplane on the basis of your opinion, please tell me which one it is, because it will never fly. Today we are celebrating truth, not your opinion. Now, come and get your diploma.

I did not give a "trigger warning" to those students before cautioning them about the danger of opinions. Nor did I provide a "safe space" where they could recover from my "microaggression."

I loved them too much to let them believe a dangerous fantasy. But that simply is not the case at most colleges and universities where the forecast calls for intense snowflake insanity.

WORSE THAN YOU THINK

The term "safe space" has been popularized by students and university ideologues to refer to a designated offense-free area where someone can "feel" comfortable and "safe" from emotional and physical harm. Yet physical harm is exactly what one professor and visiting speaker at Middlebury College experienced at the hands of the same students insisting on a safe space for their own ideas.

Protesters at this college shut down a live event featuring an interview between Middlebury Professor Allison Strange and Charles Murray, the controversial author of *The Bell Curve*. The students protested so loudly that they effectively kept anyone from listening to the presentation. After someone pulled the fire alarm, Murray and Strange were forced outside the assembly area. On their way out, they were "physically and violently confronted," according to Bill Burger, the college's vice president for communications and marketing. "The protestors then violently set upon the car, rocking it, pounding on it, jumping on and tried to prevent it from leaving campus. At one point a large traffic sign was thrown in front of the car.... One of the demonstrators pulled Prof. Stanger's hair and twisted her neck." She was taken to the hospital and wore a neck brace the following day.[4] It would seem that these snowflake students are not the ones most in need of a safe space these days.

Students at the University of California, Berkeley, created "safe spaces" in October 2016 for transgendered individuals and "people of color." White students, and presumably anyone else suspected of sympathizing with conservative views of sexuality, were blocked from passing through these "safe spaces" en route to their classes. Because a bridge was blocked, some students—those who were not "of color" or transgendered—had to cross a dry, shallow creek in order to get to class. The protesters also targeted the student store and disrupted students trying to study at the Student Union.[5]

At Notre Dame University, students affiliated with "The Fighting Irish's class of 2017" started a #NotMyCommencementSpeaker protest when Vice President Mike Pence was invited to speak. The other student groups involved in the protest were the Diversity Council and the College Democrats. One student at Notre Dame said, "...for many people on our campus, it makes them feel unsafe to have someone who openly is offensive but also demeaning of their humanity and of their life and of their identity."[6] So much for being tolerant.

Gavin McInnes, a comedian, commentator, and co-founder of Vice Media, was attacked at New York University for coming to talk to the College Republican Club on campus. The protest was organized on Facebook with the title, "Disrupt Gavin McInnes at NYU."[7] Gavin was attacked with pepper spray and attempted physical assaults by many of the protestors.

At Duquesne University, the Student Government Association is trying to prevent the Chick-fil-A restaurant chain from opening a restaurant near their college campus. *The Duke*, the school's newspaper, said, "I think it's imperative the university chooses to do business with organizations that coincide with the [university's] mission and expectations they give students regarding diversity and inclusion."[8] And yet the Catholic university's motto translated from Latin is: "It is the Spirit that gives life."

The Chick-fil-A restaurant was only coming to the campus because many students requested it.

At the University of Texas at Arlington, a homosexual student accused Thomas Klocke of harassing him. A campus administrator launched a claim against Klocke without any evidence or questioning. The dean of the school then "allegedly assigned the case to the school's associate director of academic integrity, who promptly issued an order prohibiting Klocke not only from contacting his accuser, he also prohibited him from attending the class where the incident occurred, and—crucially—from contacting any member of the class, directly or through any other person." The dean also blocked Klocke's father, who is an attorney, from hearing or being involved in anything related to the case, and prevented Klocke from contacting any witnesses who could prove his innocence. No due process. No evidence. Tragically, Klocke committed suicide.[9]

Wendy Kaminer is a free speech advocate who argues that "racist" speech in literature, like some of the language used in the book *The Adventures of Huckleberry Finn*, should not be censored. After she spoke at an alumnae event at Smith College, students protested, because the president of the college did not immediately rebuke Wendy Kaminer for using a "racist" word. They deemed her "unsafe" for students. Ms. Kaminer said she found it amazing that students could not distinguish the "difference between racist speech and discussions about racist speech."[10]

At the University of Michigan, a student activist group launched protests and petitioned to create a "designated space on central campus for Black students and students of color to organize and do social justice work."[11] The university had already built a ten million dollar multicultural center in response to student demands, but the students claimed the new center was too far from the center of campus. They insisted the new space be staffed and stocked with resources so students could organize for the sake of "social justice."

It seems the "safe space" label only applies to those voices deemed acceptable by some. On the campus of the University of Wisconsin-Madison, the Student Coalition for Progress created a petition that labeled the Young Americans for Freedom chapter as a hate group. Their crime? Inviting a speaker to discuss the use of safe spaces, trigger warnings, and microaggressions to silence free speech on college campuses! The petition accused them of "creating a hostile environment on campus."[12] The Student Coalition for Progress demanded that the members of the Young Americans for Freedom be subjected to "intensive diversity training" and asked for students to report if they felt traumatized.

During the inauguration of President Trump, a Georgetown University student group called "GUPride" organized a *"Post-inauguration self-care"* event that would be "a night of relaxation, recovery, and rest.... There will be Legos and stuffed animals and coloring books—come to embrace the inner child and hang out with people."[13] Yet when President Obama was inaugurated, twice, no "safe spaces" were needed to console conservative or Republican students with juice boxes and teddy bears.

At American University there are "stress-free zones" that allow students to escape from the stress of studying for exams. The "safe spaces" includes food, drinks, games, and "de-stress kits."[14] The sign leading to the "zone" reads, "Absolutely no studying for finals, looking at flashcards" or "calculating grades...tolerated beyond this point." The rigors of studying are, apparently, too stressful for this coddled generation. Many colleges these days are providing coloring books, snacks, and games to their students to lighten their stress levels.

This desire to create a "safe" environment has spawned the phrase "trigger warning." Certainly, when potentially offensive topics are about to be discussed, common decency assumes some advance notice be given so that any who might be offended can excuse themselves. We expect content warnings on movies and television shows or even news videos that may contain shocking images. But the use of trigger warnings on college campuses today is designed to protect students from being exposed to ideas or truths they don't want to hear. For example, before any candid discussion about sexual morality, marriage, STDs, or sexual assault, professors are now expected to issue "trigger warnings" so that those who may be offended by the discussion or those who simply don't want to be part of the classroom give and take can leave.

The Foundation for Individual Rights in Education (FIRE) has cited several colleges and universities that now require professors to warn students of potentially "triggering" language or material: Bay Path University, Colby-Sawyer College, North Iowa Area Community College, St. Vincent's College, and Drexel University, to name a few. Schools such as these have policies in place that put the onus of avoiding offense on the professor, assuming every student to be a victim-in-waiting.

But what constitutes an offense has been dumbed down and labeled a *microaggression*—and what that is exactly, is anyone's guess. Teaching students to be courteous and respectful, is one thing, but that's not what the Left is interested in, as we can see by their own student protesters. "Microaggressions" exceed the boundaries of common sense and are simply an excuse to end debates, punish dissent, and provide another rationale for leftist protests. Some campuses now prohibit expressions such as, "Everyone can succeed in this society if they work hard enough" or "America is the land of opportunity." Once considered bedrocks of American success, both statements are now deemed microaggressions that could offend those who feel they lack opportunity or success. The ideas of Plato, Aristotle, Descartes, and Russell must be purged from the curriculum on some campuses, because they were all white males.[15] Many colleges have even created "Bias Response Teams" to respond to any allegedly offensive speech on campus.[16]

Education is supposed to challenge us to reason logically and to diligently seek truth. But that's not happening with safe spaces and speech codes and the silencing of conservative dissent from the leftist orthodoxy that's endemic on college campuses.

"If you stop talking to people, you either submit to them, or you go to war with them," says Dr. Joseph Patterson of the University of Toronto. "Those are your options and those aren't good options. It's better to have a talk. If you put restrictions on speech, then you can't actually talk about the difficult things that need to be talked about." Patterson says that protecting students' feelings is "childish it's beyond comprehension. What did Nietzsche say: 'You can judge a man's spirit by the amount of truth he can tolerate." I tell my students that C. S. Lewis described the great lion, Aslan, in the Chronicles of Narnia as "not safe, but good" so too, is the "great lion" of the liberal arts: it is not supposed to be safe but surely is good! You can tell you're being well educated when you are more excited by the goodness of your character than you are in your own comfort and safety. If all ideas are "safe" then you're not learning anything. The truth is that if our universities continue to become risk-free spaces, they will soon become learning-free spaces.

3

I'LL BET YOU THINK LIFE IS ABOUT YOU

**"I CELEBRATE MYSELF, AND SING MYSELF,
AND WHAT I ASSUME YOU SHALL ASSUME."**
—WALT WHITMAN

You did get your Thanksgiving Toolkit before sitting down with family for a grateful feast last year, didn't you? The College of William and Mary provided it for students preparing to leave their coddled campus to reengage with the real world where—gasp—family members might have different opinions.

The English Department hosted "a conversation among faculty and students" to talk about "strategies for discussing privilege," showing solidarity with "those made vulnerable by the election results," providing "resources to pass on to family," and teaching students "how to deescalate conversations." The fact that faculty would think students need specific instructions on how to engage the real world when leaving campus for a week or two should tell us all we need to know about the sorry state of education. Students may be able to avoid thinking critically or debating opposing viewpoints at college, but upon returning home, parents and grandparents may not provide "safe spaces" in the kitchen or "trigger warnings" before opinions get passed along with the cranberries.

There is a deeper problem with the premise behind the "Toolkit." How self-centered must one be to go to a family holiday celebration in order to advance a political and social agenda? Who arrives with pamphlets to drop in Uncle Melvin's lap while he naps after eating too much turkey? Who concocts a holiday strategy to enlighten Grandma on transgender issues? A very self-absorbed person.

The title of the event says it all: "How to Handle Politically-Motivated Family Conflict and *Take Care of Yourself*"[emphasis mine].[1] After all, at the university these days, life *is* all about *you*. And you are *expected* to be constantly offended—even over Thanksgiving dinner with family, or for that matter over Halloween costumes.

Tantrum-throwing students besieged Yale University because Erika Christakis, a university lecturer and associate master of the school's Silliman College, sent an email to students suggesting they shouldn't be overly sensitive about Halloween costumes. Instead, Christakis encouraged students to be tolerant and avoid trying to censor expression.

"American universities were once a safe space not only for maturation but also for a certain regressive, or even transgressive, experience," she wrote. "Increasingly, it seems, they have become places of censure and prohibition."[2] As a result of her calls for tolerance, there was a student uprising calling for the resignation of Christakis and her husband Nicholas (Silliman's master). Students were recorded screaming from the campus green that the couple had made Yale a dangerous place where they felt threatened and fearful. One video showed a female undergrad confronting—with four letter words—a calm, reasoned, Dr. Nicholas Christakis, shouting at him, "It is not about creating an intellectual space! It is not! Do you understand that? It is about creating a home here!"

After weeks of unrelenting pressure, Erika and Nicolas (who is both an M.D. and a Ph.D.) resigned from their positions at Silliman College. "If healthy debate can't flourish in a university whose motto is 'light and truth,'" Erika wrote, "our problems are bigger than hurtful appropriation and cut to the heart of how a great university can contribute to a truly free and just society."[3] Erika Christakis is, ironically, an expert in early childhood education.

In March 2016, students at Emory University were offended because someone had written "Trump 2016" in chalk on a campus sidewalk. Instead of ignoring it or washing it off, protestors marched across the Emory quad shouting, "You are not listening! Come speak to us, we are in pain!" The whining students then moved into the administration building calling out, "It is our duty to fight for our freedom. It is our duty to win. We must love each other and support each other. We have nothing to lose but our chains." The university's president, Jim Wagner, met with the protesters and later sent an email to all students and faculty, saying, in part, "During our conversation, they voiced their genuine concern and pain in the face of this perceived intimidation.... After meeting with [them], I cannot dismiss their expression of feelings and concern...." No wonder they think it's all about them.

Students at Brown University became concerned when they heard a student group had organized a forum on sexual assault that would include a speaker known for being critical of the term "rape culture." "Bringing in a speaker like that could serve to invalidate people's experiences," said Kathryn Byron, a member of Brown's Sexual Assault Task Force. While Ms. Byron was meeting with school administrators to share her anxiety, other students put up posters around campus advertising that a "safe space" would be available for anyone who found the proposed debate too upsetting. The safe space would give any students who might find the debate's comments "troubling" or "triggering," a place to recuperate. The room was equipped with cookies, coloring books, bubbles, Play-Doh, calming music, pillows, blankets, and a video of frolicking puppies. One student who did actually attempt to attend the objectionable lecture felt so overwhelmed she left and hurried over to the safe space, saying, "I was feeling bombarded by a lot of viewpoints that really go against my dearly and closely held beliefs." Imagine that, encountering alternate viewpoints on a college campus.

A Columbia University student group called Everyone Allied Against Homophobia placed fliers under the door of every dorm room on campus stating, "I want this space to be a safer space." Students were asked to tape the fliers to their windows in solidarity with the LGBTQ cause. The flier was also published in the student newspaper along with an editorial asserting that "making spaces safer is about learning how to be kind to each other."

A junior named Adam Shapiro decided to respond by publishing his own message in *The Columbia Daily Spectator*. "Kindness alone won't allow us to gain more insight into truth," he wrote. In a subsequent interview, he added, "If the point of a safe space is therapy for people who feel victimized by traumatization, that sounds like a great mission.... I don't see how you can have a therapeutic space that's also an intellectual space."

THE ME, ME, ME GENERATION

It's no secret the millennial generation is thin-skinned, self-absorbed, and narcissistic—even they know it. *Time* magazine titled millennials the "Me, Me, Me Generation." The 2013 magazine cover showed a girl with her hand stretched out taking a selfie with the tag line, "Millennials are lazy, entitled, narcissists, who still live with their parents."[4] According to a 2014 poll by Reason–Rupe, 65 percent of millennials said the word *entitled* described them *well* or *somewhat well* and seven in ten millennials said the word *selfish* described them *well* or *somewhat well*.[5] A 2015 Pew survey reported millennials believe their generation is the least "moral, responsible and willing to sacrifice" when compared to Gen Xers, Baby Boomers, and the Silent Generation. When asked which generation was the most "greedy, wasteful, and self-absorbed," millennials ranked themselves number one.[6] Perhaps we can take some consolation that even in the midst of their love affair with themselves, today's youth at least retain some degree of self-awareness.

As a university president, I have a front row seat to watch hundreds of these students descend onto my college campus every year. Even on a conservative, Christian university campus such as mine, the near pathological self-centeredness of this generation is on full display. In addition to the young man I cited earlier who was offended by a chapel sermon on 1 Corinthians 13, I see the annual host of athletes whose feelings are hurt because a coach was too harsh or a practice too demanding. I see the student who fails tests repeatedly and insists it is because the professor is unfair or the requirements too stiff. I see the young man dismissed for drug possession who complains about the police rather than accepting responsibility for his own conduct. I see the student who is incredulous because a faculty member dared to penalize him for skipping class or missing an assignment. I see young people coming out of supposedly good churches and good Christian high schools who seem oblivious to one of the central axioms of Christ's message: "The first shall be last and the last shall be first." I see students who seem to sincerely believe that because they have chosen to bless us with their enrollment they deserve an A, regardless of their effort or academic performance.

Perhaps most disturbing of all, I see parents who support and defend their whining sons and daughters every step of the way. After all, little "Susie" couldn't possibly be wrong, she has a case full of participation trophies to prove it. No wonder the socialist Bernie Sanders attracted such a following on college campuses. Students have been conditioned to want someone who will level the playing field and promise to ensure approved outcomes. They want someone to make sure they win and succeed. They want someone to take all the risk out of life so they can continue coasting. But coasting can only take them in one direction—downhill.

Reflecting on the millennial generation reminds me of one of literature's classic stories: the story of Narcissus. Narcissus was the son of the river god Cephisus. He was incredibly handsome, so handsome the beautiful tree nymph, whose name was Echo, followed his every step pursuing his love.

One day after an exceptionally good hunt, Narcissus came upon a calm, clear pool of water. Exhausted and fatigued, he stooped down to take a drink and saw his own image in the water. Struck by the beauty of the reflection, Narcissus gazed with admiration and said to himself, "Not even Bacchus nor Apollo themselves surpass such allure as mine." Infatuated by what he saw, Narcissus could not tear himself away. He lost all thought of food or rest. He stayed by the river's edge day after day hovering over the pool, gazing at his own image.

As time went by, he lost his color, he lost his vigor, he lost his strength, and—in one final attempt to embrace his own fading beauty—Narcissus leaned over the edge of the pool, fell in, and drowned. In love with himself, Narcissus died leaving nothing but the faint hint of Echo's voice in a distant valley as she mourned the loss of such wasted beauty.

Today's millennials are tragically wasting away in similar fashion. Day after day, they sit at our cultural river's edge hovering over the shimmering pool of light on their iPhones and iPads. Night after night, they gaze at their own image on Facebook, Instagram, Twitter, Snapchat, and Vimeo. They can't seem to tear themselves away. And after years of having little thought of anything but themselves, they are losing their values, virtue, and character. They are about to drown in their own selfishness. The sad thing is they seem to know it.

In spite of being mesmerized by their own popularity, image, and beauty, they seem to intuitively know it is wrong and fraught with danger. But, like Narcissus, they persist. They refuse to admit what their hearts tell them: this god is an illusion. He is not real.

To be fair, the temptations millennials face today are dramatically greater than those faced by previous generations. I did not have Snapchat to share my story with the world twenty-four hours a day. I did not have Facebook to stay connected with friends from every stage of life. The opportunity to create the perfect god-like portrayal of myself wasn't available for my generation. Our fame and beauty was never achieved or affirmed through Instagram. We did not craft our careers by posting videos of ourselves on YouTube. We never imagined such things.

Millennials walk a path with trials we did not have and never dreamed of encountering.

So, while we rightly criticize them for their self-absorption, perhaps we should, at the same time, ask what role previous generations have played in creating these little demigods. Why are millennials so self-consumed? What contributed to forming them into who they are today? Does at least part of the responsibility fall upon the generations preceding them? How did we get, after all, from the Greatest Generation—meeting the challenges of an economic depression, World War II, the Korean War, and the Cold War—to the Most Self-Absorbed Generation in need of safe spaces and trigger warnings?

Much of the fault lies with education, and what happened to higher education in the 1960s. The student riots of that era led to three major, and harmful, developments: one, the purpose of college became less about learning and more about flattering the self-righteousness of students; two, the core curriculum of classics was gutted as the allegedly irrelevant or oppressive works of dead, white, males and were replaced by more "relevant" topics like women's studies and various ethnic studies, all informed by cultural Marxism; and three, many of the campus radicals of the 1960s became tenured professors and transformed their academic departments in their own image.

Predating all this, of course, was the ultimate cause. The university was a Christian invention, but over the centuries and especially in the decades of the twentieth century in our own country, it was progressively secularized. The focus in today's academia is not knowledge or character-building or truth, it is "diversity" or "tolerance," but of a very select kind, as most universities are resolutely opposed to true diversity of thought, given their speech codes and bans, and are interested in tolerance only in so far as it benefits certain favored groups.

Preaching tolerance, while at the same time dismissing truth, has led the millennial generation to embrace a moral and intellectual nihilism. If there is no objective truth and only subjective opinion, inevitably one's opinion becomes the *summum bonum* or highest good and the idea that truth exists and finding it might involve study and debate is lost.

This is, by no means, an indictment of *every* student or *every* parent. There are still thousands of good students whose parents have taught them that truth and humility, discipline and integrity are much more important than personal affirmation and selfish gain. A remnant still understands the difference between the tenuous arrogance that comes from gazing at ourselves and the unshakable confidence we find by looking to our Creator and learning about truth.

CHRONOLOGICAL SNOBBERY

I was confronted by a young man a few years ago who fancied himself a burgeoning scholar. He disagreed with what he defined as my "conservative" worldview and said, "The problem with you conservatives is that you're arrogant. You think you're always right."

I suggested to him that confidence is not the same as arrogance and that in any sincere debate both parties *think* they have the correct answer. The real dividing line is between the man who claims to be the source of truth, subjective truth, and the man who claims to be the recipient of truth, which is objective. Why is it arrogant for one man to say, "I don't have all the answers, but I believe there is an answer," and yet humble for another to proclaim, "There is no final answer. Truth is what I decide it is. I am the final judge"? One has confidence in God or some transcendent authority, the other asserts that his opinion is the only authority. So who is truly arrogant? I suggested to my young challenger that he had it backward.

My millennial friend didn't understand that the more he elevated his subjective opinions as the final standard for what is "right" the more he arrogantly diminished any meaningful debate; and when there can be no meaningful debate, arguments have to be settled by force, which is why college campuses have become such inhospitable places for conservative speakers, who are routinely shouted down, or for conservative points of view, which are often silenced.

Good education, a truly liberal education, one engaged in respectful debate and the search for truth, relies on the idea that there is a truth out there to be grasped, whether in a mathematical formula, a scientific discovery, a philosophical thesis, or a literary work that highlights a truth about the laws of nature or the nature of man.

Yet we teach college students today that they—their subjective feelings, ideas, hopes, and dreams—are the measure of all that is true and right. Consequently, many of today's millennials are not so much confident in their beliefs as they are arrogant in their opinions and disdainful of others. Our universities have become adept at churning out degrees in opinions, rather than degrees grounded in truth. We have raised a generation to be very assured of themselves while at the same time having little confidence in much else. They claim there is no truth, but then they presume to be the very source of truth when they want something to be true.

They engage in what C. S. Lewis called "chronological snobbery." They place little value in the time-tested ideas passed down to them by previous generations. The "older books" have little to offer. Many no longer turn to Sacred Scripture or the church to guide their actions, inform their morality, or inspire their beliefs. Instead, they believe they have everything they need within themselves to decide right and wrong. They believe themselves to be humble while all who dare disagree are oppressive and arrogant.

It is a common error of youth. "The arrogance of the young is a direct result of not having known enough consequences," said humorist Harry Golden. "The turkey that every day greedily approaches the farmer who tosses him grain is not wrong. It is just that no one ever told him about Thanksgiving." So it is with millennials who arrogantly presume they know all that is relevant about reality at such a young age.

C. S. Lewis defined true humility as "not thinking less of yourself," but rather as "thinking of yourself less." How far we have fallen from this ideal. One of the priorities we hold dear at my university is to teach each of our students that life is not about them. Many millennials know this intuitively. They long for something deeper, a purpose greater than themselves. For all their apparent selfishness, millennials are also the most compassionate, charity-oriented generation in history.[7] According to Leigh Buchanon in her book *Meet the Millennials*, this generation is "primed to do well by doing good. Almost 70% say that giving back and being civically engaged are their highest priorities."[8]

This is not by accident. The Greatest Generation made sacrifices to build a better life for future generations—and they largely succeeded. And while prosperity has dangers—dangers seen in the millennials—it also offers opportunities. Technology, for instance, has put charitable causes at our fingertips. And the very fact that millennials need something to counter the shallow narcissism and self-absorption that has filled their lives is an opportunity for growth and an opening for truth.

Something inside them screams, *This isn't about you*! I want millennials to know not only is life not about them but also neither is truth; we need humble hearts to see that God alone knows it all.

I want students to understand life is more about wisdom than wealth, service than selfishness, and virtue than vanity. It's about saying: "I don't have all the answers, but I believe there is one. I am willing to engage in respectful debate to pursue it." It's about repenting of the childish arrogance that led us to believe the lie: "There is no final answer. Truth is what I decide it is. I am the final judge. I am the final arbiter of what is right or wrong, true or false."

All of us, not just millennials, would do well to remember the story of Narcissus. Do we find ourselves staring lovingly at our own opinions, tastes, preferences, and desires, or do we look deeper, beyond ourselves, seeking to someday "know even as we are known"?

True education—a classical liberal education—is not about you or me. It's about learning that there is something bigger and better, more trustworthy and enduring, than what we see in the mirror. An education that truly liberates is one where the self is forgotten and a Savior is gained.

4

PRO-WOMAN—
AND PROUD OF IT!

Wellesley College is an all-girls' school. Or at least it used to be, until students who enrolled as women began transitioning to become "men." Some transitioned through hormonal "therapy" (though biological realities remain in every strand of your DNA), others simply became "gender-neutral" or "identify" as men. When one such person ran for student office, controversy erupted.

She goes by Timothy now, but when first enrolling in Wellesley, she checked off the "female" box and then indicated she was a "masculine-of-center genderqueer" person. All went well until Timothy announced she would be running for the school's office of multicultural affairs coordinator, a position to promote a "culture of diversity" on campus. Now that she identified as a *he*, and a white *he* at that, other students felt she was no longer qualified to lead at Wellesley. "I thought he'd do a perfectly fine job," said one of the students behind the campaign to keep her out, "but it just felt inappropriate to have a white man there."[1]

Such is the confused state of college campuses today that someone feels the need to justify why a man, or a woman posing as a man, should not be a student leader at an all-women's college. Not so long ago, words such as *he* and *she* had objective meaning grounded in science and facts. Now *male* and *female* are but monikers to be bent to the whims of a self-absorbed generation that places feelings above reality. Most universities today encourage students to believe reality can be bent without consequences. Yet women are put most at risk by attempts to redefine biological sex.

I won't belabor the point here that most college campuses have become sex carnivals where intercourse has replaced hand-shaking as an expected manner of greeting. Not only is this debauchery tolerated, it is celebrated and encouraged by the same students and faculty who pretend to be for the rights and the dignity of women. The sex-crazed environment on campuses today leaves women vulnerable and used, and sometimes has men running from lawsuits. I'll return later to the damage caused by the sexcapade culture on college campuses, but I want to first focus on the attacks on women promoted and encouraged by university leaders all across America in the name of "gender fluidity."

UNICORNS AND LEPRECHAUNS

In March 2016, North Carolina passed its so-called bathroom bill, overturning the ordinance of Charlotte's city council that would have forced businesses to let biological men use women's restrooms and vice versa. In response to this common sense legislation, the academic world went crazy. The National Collegiate Athletic Association (NCAA) threatened to pull all championship athletic events from the state and the National Association of Intercollegiate Athletics (NAIA) threatened to withdraw its cross-country championship. The NAIA is the athletic organization affiliated with many smaller schools, many of them religious schools, including my own Oklahoma Wesleyan University. The NAIA presents itself as being "a governing body of small athletics programs that are dedicated to character-driven intercollegiate athletics."[2]

On September 26, 2016, the NAIA Council of Presidents disregarded a nearly unanimous recommendation of its board of commissioners and athletic directors and voted to remove their national cross-country championships from the state of North Carolina. The reason? North Carolina's "HB2 legislation creates an atmosphere where discrimination potentially exists for some NAIA student-athletes and personnel." In other words, these university presidents believe the Tar Heel state should be punished for defending a woman's right to have her own bathroom.

The next day, I announced that our school would not participate in the NAIA tournament until it was restored to North Carolina. How can the NAIA claim to be an organization that champions character if its leadership so eagerly breaks its word and its contract with the state of North Carolina? How can the NAIA claim to be an organization that supports women if the leadership is so willing to deny female athletes the right to have their own showers and toilets? I was appalled by the NAIA's disregard for such basic rights.

Under a federal law known as Title IX, colleges and universities are required to ensure women's sports get equal proportional funding with men's sports. As a result, women's participation in sports has skyrocketed and, depending on the school, some men's sports—like wrestling, swimming, gymnastics, even baseball—have been cut. Title IX of course relies on the idea that there is such a thing as a woman. But if any of us can be a woman or a man, why have separate sports squads at all?

At Oklahoma Wesleyan University, we believe there is a biological reality known as a "woman." But you'd be surprised how few people agree with us in academia. Not only that, we believe in the dignity of women. We believe you can't just say you're one or mutilate yourself to become one, you have to be one. We believe women should be granted the privacy of having their own restrooms. We believe female students should be respected as women and not insulted and demeaned and even threatened by having men masquerade as women in their dorms, in their showers, or on the athletic field. That position put us at odds with the federal government, at least during the Obama administration.

In May 2016, the Obama administration issued a "Dear colleague" letter through the Department of Education to nearly every college and university in the nation. The letter argued that the Title IX law against sex discrimination applied also to "gender identity." The letter thereby implied that women had no right to their own sports or locker rooms.

Scores of universities fell over themselves to comply with the Obama administration directive. Alabama's attorney general urged his state's schools to ignore it, but nevertheless, the University of South Alabama started allowing men who identify as female to go into the women's bathrooms and locker room areas.[3]

This is pure nonsense. It requires us to deny our senses. It denies science. It denies empirical fact. It says, "I want to live in a fairytale. I want to pretend. And everyone else must cooperate with my fantasy no matter how harmful it is to myself and everyone else."

What's next for schools that still believe in science, biology, and the reality of women? The day may not be far off when schools that stand for truth will start receiving letters from other schools before athletic contests saying, "We're not going to compete against you, because you're bigots" or because they'll be sanctioned by the NCAA or NAIA.

Doubling down on this madness, in December 2015, the Human Rights Campaign (HRC) demanded that the United States Department of Education post a list of all religious colleges and universities (such as OKWU) requesting exemptions from "existing civil rights law in order to discriminate against LGBT students." They wanted to shame these schools under the pretense of protecting students' "rights." Well, I am happy to affirm that at Oklahoma Wesleyan we recognize women's rights because we recognize women, and think it would be the height of misogyny to suggest they don't even exist.

THE BIGGEST LOSERS IN THE TRANSGENDER MADNESS

George MacDonald told us, "The one principle of hell is—'I am my own. I am my own king and my own subject. *I* am the centre from which go out my thoughts; *I* am the object and end of my thoughts.... My own glory is, and ought to be, my chief care.... My judgment is the faultless rule of things. My right is—what I desire. The more I am all in all to myself, the greater I am.... The more I close my eyes to the fact that I did not make myself; the more self-sufficing I feel or imagine myself—the greater I am.'"

The claim that our identity is defined by us and not by God—that our gender is fluid and there is no such thing as a male or female—can lead to nothing but an ugly hell of our own making. It is only repentance and confession that will rescue us from this fate.

Universities that have attempted to comply with these edicts are ignoring truth and basic common sense. The University of Iowa was one of the first to require faculty and staff to refer to students by their preferred "names and gender pronouns." Instead of a professor referring to a student as *he* or *she*, the professor refers to the student using the incorrect grammar form *they* unless the student has specified a preferred pronoun. There is also a range of invented pronouns from which students can choose, including *ze*, *zem*, *zir* or *hir*, *zirs* or *hirs*.

University president Bruce Harreld posted a video to YouTube to help promote the new policy. "My pronouns are he, him, and his," he said. "Don't make assumptions. Help us make the University of Iowa as inclusive and affirming as possible."[4] The University of Michigan enacted a similar policy; in response, a conservative student declared he prefers to be called "His Majesty." It's not clear the administration understood the joke.[5]

One day I received a letter from a woman I'll call Susan. She revealed that she had been listening to me talk about these issues of gender and sexuality on the radio for some time. She wrote to tell me I was right and to say thank you for speaking truth. She was in the process of transitioning to identify as a man, complete with hormonal therapy, and living with a man who was in the process of identifying as a woman. There may have been a time when what I said offended her, but she had come to see I was right.

At first, I suspected the letter was a ruse. But a week or two later, I went to our cafeteria on a Sunday afternoon, when local folks often come to eat good food after church. An older lady came running up, hugged me and said, "I've been coming for weeks and hoping to see you here. My daughter is Susan, the one who wrote you the letter." I couldn't have been happier. As we sat down and talked more, she said, "Susan's back home. She's returned to her faith and she's living with us again. She's been here for the last couple of weeks hoping to see you. Will you be here next week?"

The next week I entered the cafeteria and was delighted to meet Susan in person. She had a short haircut, and a bit of five o'clock shadow because of the hormone therapy, but she was obviously trying to dress in a feminine fashion. I was amazed to learn it was her partner who encouraged her to start listening to me. Both he and she were conservative on most issues, but not sexuality. "We listened to you week in and week out. He hasn't changed, but I recognized you were telling the truth. I'm back home to Christ. I'm reclaiming and affirming my biological identity."

It breaks my heart to think of the insanity going on in the world that is encouraged on nearly all college campuses today. Yet the story of Susan is an example of the freedom that can come from speaking truth with clarity and confidence and without apology. Susan has been set free by truth. She knows her identity is grounded in facts. She is not a "fluid construct" that ebbs and flows with her every fantasy. She is real. She is not make believe. She is the *imago Dei*. She is not the imago dog. Her personhood is anchored in the image of God. She is a human being with free will and moral culpability. She is not an animal held subject to her baser appetites, instincts, and inclinations.

5

CORRUPTED AND COMPROMISING CHRISTIAN UNIVERSITIES

N ote to Christian parents: don't assume that because a college has "Christian" in its name or on its four-color brochure that the faculty and leadership share your beliefs. In all likelihood, they do not.

It pains me to point to Samford University, because until last year our school and Samford were both part of the Council of Christian Colleges and Universities (CCCU). The CCCU is an organization comprised of both Protestant and Catholic schools and allegedly committed "to advance the cause of Christ-centered higher education and to help our institutions transform lives by faithfully relating scholarship and service to biblical truth." I'll explain why I say *allegedly* later in this chapter—and why OKWU is no longer a member school of CCCU. But students at Samford got a taste of how confusing Christian campuses can be these days.

When students there tried to launch a local chapter of Young Americans for Freedom, faculty leaders blocked their request, insisting the group amend the "inflammatory language" in its purpose statement, the original founding document of the group that dates back to 1960. What horrific hate speech might they have been referring to? The statement denounces the evils of communism, calling for "victory, rather than co-existence with this menace." Faculty thought this could offend members of the communist club—even though the school didn't appear to *have* a communist club. Students were actually told by faculty that they were not being kind to those with a communist background.[1]

I find it more than a bit ironic that members of the faculty at a Christian college would call for co-existence with communism, an ideology that calls for the eradication of religion. A Samford University official wrote, "This is the direct statement from the Sharon Statement [a seminal document adopted in 1960 by a group of young conservatives led by William F. Buckley Jr. It has been recognized by many historians as one of the most important declarations in the history of American conservatism.] that, though likely appropriate in 1960, does not hold the same in 2016." Truth, apparently, changes with time.

For the record, I welcome Young Americans for Freedom to come to OKWU to form a local chapter. We still believe in archaic concepts like good and evil. We stand with these young conservatives. We stand with those who suffered under communism, including the more than one hundred million people slaughtered in its name in the twentieth century. We stand with truth, no matter how that stand makes anyone feel. But uncompromising Christian universities like ours are becoming rare.

THE PATH OF CHRISTIAN COLLEGES AND UNIVERSITIES

I wrote my doctoral dissertation at Michigan State University on the shifting meaning of the word *evangelical* in modern Christianity. MSU makes no claim to be a religious school. I began my dissertation with a true story from my experience, in which a faculty member at the Christian college I was then working for confronted a student who didn't know the answer to a question in class by saying, "Jesus Christ, don't you know the answer to the question!" When I shared this story with the MSU faculty assigned to review my dissertation, they were shocked that such behavior would happen at a university that claimed to be an evangelical Christian institution. The MSU faculty disagreed with me on any number of issues and certainly shared no affinity for my conservative Christianity, yet even they intuitively recognized the incongruity between belief and practice.

Imagine how it would be received if a student at a Muslim university (rare though they may be) took Mohammed's name in vain. Unbelievably, the provost at this Christian school defended that faculty member to me by saying, "Some members of this denomination don't consider this to be cursing." I suppose I shouldn't have been so surprised since the same provost intentionally removed the word *evangelical* from job postings for new faculty because he "wanted to attract a broader base." Apparently, his efforts were successful.

Recently, a top administrator at another Christian college rejected the idea of putting a picture of students praying on the cover of the institution's alumni magazine, because "it would make too many people nervous." When a Christian college in the Midwest asked its faculty, staff, administration, and board members to define what made for a truly evangelical school, one board member specifically rejected the idea that traditional Christian sexual standards had anything to do with this, telling me, "I have searched forever and cannot find any psychological proof that sexual relationships outside of marriage are harmful.... I don't think it is a non-issue, but I don't know if it's an issue we need to have a formal position on." I wondered where she did her searching, because the vast volume of medical and sociological data and the plain teaching of the Bible, let alone what one reads in the newspaper, could have told her otherwise.

I asked another long-standing faculty leader at a respected, conservative Christian college, "What do the words *Evangelical Christian* mean to you with regard to the virgin birth, the death, the Resurrection, and the miracles of Jesus?" He answered with a straight face, "Those can be message statements. They don't need to be reality statements."

A few years ago, I received from yet another Christian college a forty-three-page, four-color publication in which the institution never once mentioned the name of Jesus. The best this college could do in these forty-three pages was to talk about education for "ethics, leadership, values, and integrity." Either they forgot to talk about Jesus, or they intentionally omitted Our Lord's name. In either case, this Christian college has clearly strayed far from its mission.

More recent headlines reveal their straying is not an isolated incident. Students enrolled in a world religions course at Texas Christian University were expected to attend a service at a Muslim mosque—on Good Friday, no less. The course syllabus required every student to attend.[2]

For Valentine's Day 2017, another Christian university of the Wesleyan tradition cancelled all classes for a day to sponsor events promoting "social justice." They called it the "Day of Courageous Conversations," including sessions such as "Supporting Even When We Don't Understand," a "Racial Injustice Bus Tour," and a "Privilege Walk."[3] For each session attended, students were entered in a drawing for a $1,000 scholarship. At Oklahoma Wesleyan University, we canceled classes a couple of weeks earlier where we hosted world-renowned apologists and scholars from Great Britain and the United States on our campus to teach our students how to give a defense for the Christian faith and embrace a biblical worldview. One Christian school teaches its students apologetics, the other teaches its students how to apologize and embrace political correctness.

At the University of San Diego, a Catholic school, black and LGBTQ students demanded that administrators denounce a Catholic saint and remove his name from a campus building because of his "colonialist legacy." Not surprisingly, other demands included adding "gender-neutral" bathrooms.[4]

BE CAREFUL WHERE YOU SEND YOUR KIDS TO SCHOOL

In my experience interacting behind the scenes with Christian university leaders, there are three kinds of Christian schools:

1. Christian in name or heritage only. These schools might retain references to the faith in their name or their official seals or even their bylaws and policy statements, but in practice they have openly left orthodox Christianity behind, and eagerly accommodate the secular liberal relativism that is the academic norm.

2. Christian in appearance but not substance. These are perhaps the most pernicious universities—they advertise themselves to parents and students as being faithful to Scripture and historic Christian belief, yet routinely hire faculty who teach unbiblical and anti-Christian doctrines to students.

These colleges are quick to show parents their Bible curriculum, but reluctant to share the course of studies from the sociology or Western literature classes for fear of exposing their anti-Christian bias. Within this group there is a broad range of schools, some more obvious in their deception than others. But parents should not believe all they see or read in the brochures. Few Christian universities require their faculty to hold the beliefs the institution officially espouses.

Let me be clear on this. I want my faculty to teach the inerrancy of Scripture and the historical veracity of the biblical worldview *while presenting opposing points of view.* Just as I want my students to understand the LGBTQ argument better than anyone else, *and to understand the biblical response to it.* In both cases, I want our teachers to leave no doubt that we are a Christian university that believes in the inerrancy of Scripture and a biblical worldview. Good education highlights counterpoints and embraces conversation, but it also involves closure. It recognizes that for questions to have any meaning and worth there must be an answer.

To me, that's good teaching—highlighting truth in a process of debate. But what often happens on Christian campuses is that teachers give little attention to the traditional side of the debate and instead emphasize and even encourage the progressive and popular view. Many Christian schools make little effort to teach their students to embrace a sound apologetic. Rather than catechize their students in the truths of Christianity, they in fact teach the opposite, implying that truth is relative and that Christianity is fraught with error.

3. Christian in word and in deed. This list of faithful Christian schools is quite short. I will not presume to give it, as events have been changing so rapidly. I know our university and a handful of others stand in this space, deeply committed to remaining true to the Christian faith—no matter the consequences. But there are fewer and fewer standing with us. Even many who do, choose to keep their heads down to avoid controversy. Many Christian universities, both Protestant and Catholic, are trying to find some middle ground. But as my next story indicates, there comes a time for choosing.

I have a litmus test at OKWU. Nobody gets hired unless they are pro-life and pro-marriage. If you want to work with us, you must also be deeply committed to the inerrancy of Scripture and the objectivity of truth. You don't get hired as a faculty member unless you understand you don't define life, God does; that marriage should be controlled by the Church and not the government; and truth is given by God and not made up by you.

Bottom line, if you can't check the boxes for the primacy of Jesus Christ, the priority of Scripture, the pursuit of truth, and the practice of wisdom, you don't get hired. If you don't believe Jesus is the Son of God, the Bible is the word of God, the truth is given by God, and obedience and integrity are demanded by God, this is the wrong place for you.

Sadly, that is not true at many universities that purport to be Christian. It's not even true at many institutions that come from the same Wesleyan tradition as OKWU. I know for a fact that several schools in my tradition don't ask prospective faculty what their views of truth and Scripture are. They don't ask if they are pro-life or pro-choice. They don't bother to thoroughly vet future professors on the issues of human identity and the exclusivity of the Christian faith. Do they still hire orthodox Christians as faculty? Sure—along with "progressives" who were never asked specific questions about the inerrancy of Scripture, the definition of life, and the objectivity of truth.

THE CCCU DEBACLE

Within days of the Supreme Court's *Obergefell* ruling on marriage in 2015, two colleges that were long standing members of the Council of Christian Colleges and Universities announced they would begin hiring married, homosexual couples. The universities were Goshen College and Eastern Mennonite University, which were charter members of the Council, so CCCU had to respond. The CCCU represents about 140 institutions of higher learning that self-identify as "Christ-centered." These colleges and universities represent approximately 450,000 students, 30,000 faculty, and 1.8 million alumni. The CCCU's mission as stated on its official website is, "To advance the cause of Christ-centered higher education and to help our institutions transform lives by faithfully relating scholarship and service to biblical truth."

Immediately after receiving word from Goshen and Eastern Mennonite that they intended to affirm the *Obergefell* decision by hiring faculty who were actively engaged in homosexual behavior, the CCCU President Shirley Hoogstra sent a note to all the member college presidents saying it was a time for consultation, dialogue, and deliberation over this issue. To his great credit, Dr. Dub Oliver, president of Union University in Tennessee, saw no need for deliberation and withdrew his school immediately. Within days, I notified Dr. Hoogstra that I intended to show solidarity with Union University and withdraw OKWU's membership from the CCCU if she (Dr. Hoogstra) did not immediately disavow Eastern Mennonite and Goshen's affirmation of gay marriage and homosexual behavior.

It was my strong belief that this situation called for a decision and not "dialogue." I felt it was time for the CCCU to demonstrate a commitment to biblical clarity as opposed to engaging in a prolonged "conversation." Scripture, in my view, is unequivocal on this issue, and I made it quite clear we should say so. Furthermore, I knew that my silence might be interpreted as acceptance, and give legitimacy to Eastern Mennonite and Goshen's decision. That was something I would not do.

When I challenged Dr. Hoogstra as to how an organization advertising itself as "biblically faithful" could possibly have a "conversation" about a sexual act specifically prohibited in Scripture, she responded by telling me "the CCCU is a broad multi-denominational organization that has members that disagree on a variety of issues such as the women's role at the pulpit, speaking in tongues and methods of baptism...." She went on to say, "In the same spirit we need to have a conversation about this issue...." And thus, this Christian leader, who is entrusted with the hearts and minds of tens of thousands of our Christian college students, actually conflated a doctrinal dispute over how one should be baptized—which can legitimately be debated—with the unmistakable, undebatable (in biblical terms) sin of sodomy.

After telling Dr. Hoogstra I took great umbrage with her attempt to place a disagreement over speaking in tongues on the same moral plane as a dispute over a biblically prohibited sexual act, I went further to say I didn't see anywhere in Scripture where we're told to sit around and have a "conversation" about sin. Exactly where is it that Jesus tells us to engage in "dialogue" and "consultation" about sexual immorality? I see him confronting it and expecting us to confess it and stop it, but I don't see any-where in the Bible where he tells us to have a "conversation" about it.

I gave Dr. Hoogstra and the CCCU thirty days to publicly state a biblically faithful position and told her that, if they did not do so, OKWU could not remain a member in good faith. When they did not alter their position, I submitted a letter with-drawing OKWU's membership. Three other schools eventually left as well, but of the 140-some colleges and universities repre-sented by the CCCU, only five saw fit to take a stand on this issue. Only five believed it was important to say the Church defines marriage, not the government, and the Bible defines sexual morality, not Eastern Mennonite University, not Goshen College, and not the CCCU.

It should be noted that after the lengthy time of "dialogue," "consultation," and "conversation," called for by the CCCU that this organization officially changed its membership status levels to now include a third category known as "collaborative part-ners." This additional classification was specifically created to welcome institutions affirming homosexual behavior (and gay marriage) into the CCCU tent. The leadership of the council makes it clear this third category doesn't have voting rights. They're saying it's not even membership. Hogwash! Call it what you will, but they have now affirmed schools that embrace homosexual behavior as acceptable "partners" in an organiza-tion that portends to "faithfully relate scholarship and service to biblical truth." If you don't think the camel just got his nose in the tent, wait a couple of years. He'll have his whole butt under the canopy soon—and it's not going to be pretty.

One of the questions I was asked during that time of "con-versations" was whether I could find it acceptable for Goshen or

EMU to retain any level of membership in the CCCU. I said *no*. Yet 30 percent of my peers—30 percent!—said *yes*. Three out of ten of the presidents of the CCCU, Christ-centered, "Bible-believing" liberal arts colleges in America said a school celebrating sodomy by affirming gay marriage could retain and enjoy membership within the organization. By the time the dust settled, no more than a handful of schools withdrew from the CCCU over its celebration of homosexual marriage and it appears that nearly all of the current members seem to be satisfied with the "compromise" of adding a category of "collaborative partners" who affirm and celebrate immoral sexual behavior at their respective schools. That speaks volumes about the state of Christian higher education in America today.

6

IDEAS HAVE CONSEQUENCES

As students at Ohio State University walked to class on a chilly November morning in 2016, Abdul Artan plowed his vehicle into them. He then jumped from the vehicle and began slashing and stabbing them with a butcher knife.[1] Police officers killed him before he could do more than injure eleven students. A Muslim student from Somalia, Artan posted Facebook rants prior to the attack that revealed it to be an act of jihad. A self-described news agency of ISIS called him "a soldier of the Islamic state." How would an esteemed university respond to such a violent act of terrorism?

Instead of teaching their students how to protect themselves against radical Islamic terrorists or encouraging them to resist radical ideologies that promote death and destruction, the Ohio State University administration invited Nathan Lean to campus. Lean is the author of *The Islamophobia*

Industry: How the Right Manufactures Fear of Muslims. He spoke on the "pernicious phenomenon" of Islamophobia.[2] The school's website claimed Lean would offer "key insights on how students, scholars, and members of the community at large can counter instances of prejudice and help realize a world that values pluralism and diversity."[3] Can one even imagine President Franklin Roosevelt taking to the radio airwaves in response to the bombing of Pearl Harbor to announce a forum on diversity and prejudice? Snowflake insanity.

Instead of addressing the attack as an act of terrorism, the university decided to use the opportunity to advance a social agenda inconsistent with reality. It only got worse from there. In the days after the attack, protestors gathered on campus to read the names of "people of color" who were killed by police officers in the previous two months.[4] Abdul Artan made the list—from terrorist to victim in a matter of weeks. On top of that irony, Artan the terrorist was enrolled in a class, with a paper due that week, about "microaggressions." As an immigrant he had not been taught to embrace American values, he had been taught to take offense at everything as a member of a preferred identity group.[5] How did it come to this? *Ideas have consequences.*

A TRAIN TO SOMEWHERE

Every year for the past decade or so during the Christmas season, I have watched the movie *The Polar Express*. I started this tradition with my sons when they were young and it has become an annual ritual ever since. As you likely know, the digitally animated production stars Tom Hanks as the conductor of a train (The Polar Express) that takes its passengers on a magical Christmas Eve trip to the North Pole.

All along the way, the children on the journey must decide if they "believe" in Christmas. One boy in particular has his doubts. Is Christmas real or just make-believe? The train ride represents his struggle. Near the end of the movie, the conductor turns to the boy and says, "The one thing about trains: It doesn't matter where you're going. What matters is deciding to get on."

As I watch the movie, I can't help but think of today's academy and the popular paradigm called "post-modern constructivism" that prevails on most of today's campuses. This model asserts that individuals in conversation with one another construct reality. There is no Truth with a capital "T" but only personal "truths" that are created uniquely by each individual as the culminating synthesis of tolerance and dialogue. It is the journey that matters, not the destination.

The constructivist's goal is to build a personal belief system, not to seek and discover immutable facts. There is no such thing as a final answer. It really doesn't matter what worldview you choose as long as you choose one that works for you. To travel is better than to arrive. Just "get on"—and any old train will do. "It doesn't matter what you believe as long as it works for you…" This commitment to radical relativism is why our judges can't find the word *marriage* in the dictionary, because to define it in the traditional Christian way is judgmental.

This is why our State Department thinks the way to stop terrorists is to give them jobs, because really all anyone ever needs is a welfare program; there is no such thing as evil. This is why our universities say they appreciate the "legitimate grievances" of Muslims who stone women, behead journalists, and crucify children, because they have their values and we have ours, and it is ignorant, wrong, and oppressive to impose our values—especially if they're Christian—on others.

History, however, teaches us the premise that all ideas are equal is pure nonsense. Yes, education does involve dialogue and discussion and, of course, we do build knowledge on the foundation of debating all worldviews and all ideas. But a classical liberal arts education (one validated by nearly one thousand years of tradition) is more than just the process of choosing from a smorgasbord of personal values and various worldviews.

A truly liberal education is one that liberates. It liberates mankind from the consequences of those things that are wrong and frees us to live within the beauty of those things that are right. Education grounded in the pursuit of truth as opposed to man's constructs will ultimately free us from the oppression of lies.

Education at its best serves as a light to those who are in the dark. It is a map to those who are lost. It is a law to those who want order. When we are driven by the hunger for answers rather than the protection of opinions, we are not afraid to put all ideas on the table, because we have confidence that, in the end, we can embrace what is true and right and discard what is false and wrong. Confident in the existence of truth, we recognize we should find the right "train" going in the "right" direction.

Another movie also features a train ride. This train, however, was not leading to the magical snow-filled skies of the North Pole but instead to the ash-laden horror of Auschwitz and Dachau. Steven Spielberg's *Schindler's List* demonstrates that it does, indeed, matter which train one chooses to get on. In the moving masterpiece, the fallacy of post-modern constructivism comes alive—and dies—before our eyes.

Who can watch fellow human beings herded as cattle into boxcars bound for the furnaces of the Nazi prison camps and argue that it doesn't matter where the train is going? Who would dare tell the Jews the joy is in the journey and the destination is of little consequence? Some "trains" lead to good and some "trains" lead to evil. We should all want to avoid getting on the wrong train, and weep, as Oskar Schindler weeps, for those headed in the wrong direction.

Just as trains have destinations, so do ideas. Why would we expect decades of teaching sexual promiscuity in our schools to result in sexual restraint in our students? Why are we surprised at the selfishness of our culture when we have immersed several generations of our children in a curriculum that teaches self-esteem more effectively than it does science and civics? How can we possibly think teaching values clarification rather than moral absolutes will result in a virtuous people? We seem to think education is about acquiring more information than embracing more ethics. The academy has lost its way and as a consequence our culture is losing its sense and we are in danger of losing our souls.

WORSHIPPING THE CREATED

In the early 1900s, G. K. Chesterton spoke of the unavoidable consequences of denying God as our creator and worshipping science above the sacred. Observing that the naturalists of his day were only too willing to turn their science into a philosophy and then impose their new religion upon all of culture with near fanatic zeal, Chesterton said, "I [have] never said a word against eminent men of science. What I complain of is a vague popular philosophy which supposes itself to be scientific when it is really nothing but a sort of new religion and an uncommonly nasty one."

Recognizing that science could never presume to compete in the moral arena of theology and philosophy, Chesterton went further, "To mix science up with philosophy is only to produce a philosophy that has lost all its ideal value and a science that has lost all its practical value. It is for my private physician to tell me whether this or that food will kill me. It is for my private philosopher to tell me whether I ought to be killed." Chesterton knew science could answer the questions of mathematics and medicine, but he, likewise, was keenly aware it had nothing at all to say about meaning and morality. He warned that scientific "progress" unrestrained by sacred principles was fraught with dangers. "Survival of the fittest," he contended, may be an interesting academic discussion when applied to a vegetable, an animal, or a mineral, but when practiced on people, its consequences are nothing short of horrifying.

C. S. Lewis also spoke forthrightly of Western society's diminishment of God while elevating man and technology to fill the void. Predicting the rise of what he and others labeled "scientism," where naturalism and materialism would be uncritically elevated to the status of a religion, Lewis warned of a dystopia where public policy and even moral and religious beliefs would be dictated by professors and politicians only too eager to assume the role of our new cultural high priests.

In his novel titled *That Hideous Strength*, Lewis asks the reader to consider an obvious question: after two world wars in which scientism has brought us the "advancements" of eugenics and the mass slaughter of millions of people via poisonous gas, rapid fire machine guns, ballistic rockets, and atomic bombs, how is our new manmade god working for us?

"The physical sciences, good and innocent in themselves, [have] already…begun to be warped," said Lewis. "[They have] been subtly maneuvered in a certain direction. Despair of objective truth [has] been increasingly insinuated into the scientists [or the cultural elites]; indifference to it, and a concentration upon mere power, [has] been the result...."[6] Lewis knew the struggle by the "fittest" for power and survival, when unhampered by any objective moral restraint, would always lead to the nightmare of Orwellian rule rather than the paradise promised by his professorial peers, and he cautioned his readers accordingly.

The list of those warning of the inevitable consequences of worshipping the created rather than the Creator is long. Chesterton, Lewis, J. R. R. Tolkien, T. S. Eliot, and many more, both before and after them, all knew that when man reverses the equation of Creator and created and, thus, denies God as his origin, humanity always suffers dire consequences.

Chuck Colson, the late founder of the Colson Center for Christian Worldview, summarized it well: "Our origin determines our destiny. It tells us who we are, why we are here, and how we should order our lives together in society. Our view of origins shapes our understanding of ethics, law, [and] education...Whether we start with the assumption that we are creatures of a personal God or that we are products of a mindless process, a whole network of consequences follows, and these consequences diverge dramatically."[7]

If we are the intentional design of an intelligent creator, then we have a purpose, a destiny, and a way in which to live our lives in order to fulfill that purpose. If we are nothing more than products of happenstance and chance, then we have no ultimate purpose and meaning and no standard to guide the way we are to live our lives. Morality becomes meaningless and right and wrong are nothing more than social constructs—subject to the whim and opinion of those who position themselves to have the most power.

As Colson said, in such a world any claim to universal truth is considered suspect, especially if it claims its source in God rather than human understanding and accomplishment.[8] In such a world, lies always fill the vacuum vacated by truth. When we think we are our own creators, there is little left for us to do but worship ourselves. Life really does become all about us. Education becomes little more than the formalization of self-worship. As T. S. Eliot stated, "Every definition of the purpose of education…implies some concealed or rather implicit, philosophy or theology. In choosing one definition rather than another we are attracted to the one because it fits better with our answer to the question: What is man for?"[9]

ALL THEY NEED IS A LITTLE TLC

By the middle of the twentieth century, many educators had embraced a new paradigm that changed American education in a profound way. Instead of the millennia-old view of mankind being created by God and prone to sin, a new belief was adopted that emphasized children were, instead, merely the evolutionary products of nature and nurture. They were basically "good" and would flourish accordingly if given the optimal amount of positive reinforcement and tender loving care. Education, therefore, shifted from discipline, structure, and moral training to simply giving students more attention and more affirmation. Believing all children were essentially blank slates progressing along the evolutionary chain of self-actualization with no predisposition toward selfishness, teachers began restructuring the curriculum and the classroom to encourage rather than confront, and compliment rather than correct.

Labeling any action as *sinful* was viewed as harmful to a child's self-worth and emotional development. All that was necessary to create a perfect child was a perfect environment, and, thus, the birth of an ideology of utopian thinking where the village supplanted the parent in raising the child. For if our children are basically good at birth, then all that's needed for the realization of our brave new world is for the smarter ones—the brighter oligarchy of elites—to design a society that seamlessly provides the optimal amount of comfort and care to encourage our precious little flowers to bloom and grow in the bright sun of a professor's sagacity and a politician's social engineering.

By the 1960s and 1970s, these ideas were being lived out nationwide. As Chuck Colson says, parents became "sympathetic therapists" instead of "stern moralizers."[10] Many churches began to abdicate their educational responsibility. Many pastors bought into the progressive lie that education was best left to government schools and the church should only concern itself with "spiritual growth" of its parishioners. When it came to educating our kids, God was out and government was in. With very little protest, a country that still defined itself as a "Christian nation" ceded the responsibility of educating an entire generation to a secular system that was, and is, antithetical to Christian virtues.

THE POWER OF IDEAS

When addressing the nation on the issue of Islamic terrorism in 2015, President Obama said he believed "ideologies are not defeated with guns, they are defeated with better ideas."[11] I agree.

Perhaps Mr. Obama and those who share his worldview should consider some of their own ideas. Ideas such as proclaiming with narcissistic confidence "we are the ones we've been waiting for," and "we are the change we seek," that killing unborn babies is a morally neutral choice, and our sex is whatever we deem it to be.

Ideas matter. It matters when we teach young men to view young women as nothing but objects of recreation and young women to accept this insult. It matters when we teach our children a career is more important than character and money is more important than morality. It matters when we teach students there is no God—and treat them as if *they* are gods.

C. S. Lewis once warned us that severing men from morality is akin to "removing the organ and yet demanding the function," like thinking you can "geld the stallion and bid him be fruitful." Most everyone wants a "moral" society, but we can't have one if we can't agree on what morality means. Virtually our entire system of higher education is dedicated to the idea that Christian morality is passé if not oppressive, and that we each should define our own morality along the Left's approved racial, sexual, or class categories. That's the direction higher education is taking our culture—and even at Christian colleges few seem to want to stop it. But at Oklahoma Wesleyan, we most definitely do.

GOOD IDEAS PRODUCE GOOD TEACHING

I received an early Christmas present in 2010. It came in the form of a headline run by CBS *Money Watch* and *The Huffington Post*: "Oklahoma Wesleyan University ranked number one with the best university professors in the entire nation."[12] A conservative Christian college gets cited by the mainstream media as having the "best faculty in the nation"! Not Harvard. Not Dartmouth. Not my alma mater, Michigan State University. But Oklahoma Wesleyan University. We have stayed at or near the top of that list ever since.

How did this happen? Good teaching presupposes good ideas, and we offer both. None of our students graduate with a degree in "whatever;" our students earn degrees in real academic disciplines where they are challenged and held to the highest standards. Above all, our goal, as the Psalmist says, is, "Teach me your way, O LORD, that I may walk in your truth" (Psalm 86:11).[13] That is what higher education lacks above all else—and that is what is corrupting our culture—a refusal to pursue truth. Without that, we are a nation truly lost.

7

THE PRODIGAL UNIVERSITY

In November 2015 two things were reported to have happened at the University of Missouri. First, the Mizzou student body president said he saw someone drive through campus in a red pickup, hurling racial slurs. Second, this same young man claimed he witnessed the KKK somewhere on campus and felt his safety was threatened. The problem: neither of these incidents was ever confirmed and, in fact, the second was later retracted and followed by a public apology.

But retractions and apologies aside, these reports brought protestors to the University of Missouri campus chanting, "No justice, no peace, white silence is violence." The Black Lives Matter group held a "sit-in" at the campus library for two days. Eventually, to satisfy these demonstrators the administration implemented mandatory "diversity and inclusion training for all faculty, staff, and students."[1] Any students who did not complete the training could not enroll in classes. The training claimed to "create awareness of and address [the] conscious and unconscious discrimination" that existed between the students, faculty, and staff of the university.

This was not enough to satisfy the protesters, however. Eventually, the president and provost lost their jobs under pressure that they had not done enough to address the students' concerns. Thus these students, along with the compliant faculty and administration at the University of Missouri, helped destroy the very idea of a university. When universities were created in the Middle Ages they represented a united body of students and teachers pursuing truth. The University of Missouri—and most other universities around the country—has rejected truth and unity in favor lies and division.

The sad tale of the University of Missouri's departure from its true mission is a reminder of how American higher education is like the prodigal son. It had a great inheritance and squandered it. Unlike the prodigal son, it has yet to come home.

American higher education, from its inception during the Puritan era until the end of the nineteenth century, was established and operated within the context of a Christian ethos.[2] The guiding philosophy was "to propagate knowledge and to prepare upright leadership within a Christian society."[3] The mission of the academy during this time was not so much the advancement of scientific research but rather the promotion of moral development and civic responsibility. Professors were devoted teachers and role models, and courses in moral philosophy often served as the culmination of the college curriculum.[4] The purpose of the academy was to "confirm the traditional Protestant cosmology: the existence of God and his relationship with the world and with mankind."[5]

According to J. D. Hunter in *Evangelicalism: The Coming Generation*, "Theoretically and ideally, higher education [played] an important role in the maintenance of the moral order of orthodox Protestantism. When under the auspices of devoted believers, it [had] the purpose of galvanizing the commitment of its future leaders...and a sizable portion of its rank and file membership. It [had] the potential of making the faithful better equipped to handle the challenges of defending the faith from error and extending the influence and witness of the faith in the larger world."[6]

This "birthright" and "inheritance" of American higher education can easily be seen in the original mottos of many of our nation's most seminal institutions: Harvard's *Christo et Ecclesia*, "For Christ and the Church"; Princeton's *Vitam Mortuis Reddo*, "I restore life to the dead"; and Yale's expressed goal for its students, "to know God in Jesus Christ and....to lead a Godly, sober life." These first three American universities were unquestionably charted as Christian institutions. Harvard was founded and funded by a minister, John Harvard. Its expressed mission was to "let every Student be plainly instructed, and earnestly pressed to consider well, the main end of his life and studies is, to know God and Jesus Christ which is eternal life (John 17:3) and therefore to lay Christ in the bottom, as the only foundation of all sound knowledge and learning."[7]

Yale was established by the Church. Led by the Reverend James Pierpont, it declared its purpose: "To plant and under ye Divine blessing to propagate in this Wilderness, the blessed Reformed, Protestant Religion, in ye purity of its Order and Worship."[8] Its students were required to "live religious, godly and blameless lives according to the rules of God's Word, diligently reading the Holy Scriptures, the fountain of light and truth; and constantly attend upon all the duties of religion, both in public and secret." Prayer was a requirement. Princeton's early presidents included some of America's foremost religious leaders, including revivalist preacher Jonathan Edwards and John Witherspoon, a signer of the Declaration of Independence. Its purpose could not have been clearer: "Cursed is all learning that is contrary to the cross of Christ."[9]

Seven of the eight Ivy League institutions were founded in like manner to train up future generations in a biblical ethic; to educate a moral citizenry, and, thus, lay the foundation for a free people and a free nation. Dartmouth was founded to "Christianize" the native American tribes and its motto even to this day is *Vox clamantis in deserto*: "The voice of one crying in the wilderness."[10] Evangelist George Whitfield originally conceived the University of Pennsylvania. Three-fourths of its original trustees were affiliated with the Church of England. Its motto is *Leges Sine Moribus Vanae*: "Laws without morals [are] useless."[11] Brown university was founded by Baptists with the motto, *In Deo Speramus* which means "In God We Hope."[12] Columbia University was inspired by the dream of Colonel Lewis Morris, who wrote a letter to the Society for the Propagation of the Gospel in Foreign Parts, the missionary arm of the Church of England, arguing that New York City was an ideal community in which to establish a college for such purposes. The university's motto is taken directly from Psalm 36:9, *In lumine Tuo videbimus lumen:* "In Thy light shall we see light."[13]

The list could go on and on and literally cover coast to coast. Amherst College: *Terras Irradient*—"Let them enlighten the lands." Wellesley College: *Non Ministrari sed Ministrare*—"Not to be served, but to serve / Not to be ministered unto, but to minister." Northwestern University: *Quaecumque Sunt Vera*—"Whatsoever

things are true." Kenyon College: *Magnanimiter Crucem Sustine*—
"Valiantly bear the cross!" Ohio University: *Religio Doctrina Civilitas, Prae Omnibus Virtus*—"Religion, Learning, Civility; Above All, Virtue." Indiana University: *Lux et Veritas*—"Light and Truth." Emory University: *Cor prudentis possidebit scientiam*—"The wise heart seeks knowledge." Valparaiso University: *In luce tua videmus lucem*—"In Thy light we see light." The University of Southern California: *Palmam qui meruit ferat*—"Let whoever earns the palm bear it." The University of California: *Fiat Lux*—"Let there be light."

A friend of mine once challenged leaders at Northwestern University to explain the origin of the words that appeared on their university shield: "Whatever is true, whatever is noble, whatever is right, whatever is good." They could not. They had no idea that their university shield quoted the Bible's admonition to "think on these things."

The above institutions are just a few of hundreds that explicitly cite a Judeo-Christian ethic, or even specific biblical passages, as their guiding ethos and their very reason for existence. America's higher educational inheritance is, indeed, rich with the assumption that the highest goal of the academy should be to teach and model personal integrity within the context of God's objective truths: truths such as respect for law, a desire for virtue, a heart for sacrifice, and the value of sobriety, religion, morality, and biblical wisdom.

LEAVING HOME

In the latter half of the nineteenth century, however, higher education started its departure from these founding principles. Millions of dollars from wealthy benefactors, and the burgeoning involvement of the federal government, helped establish many new universities and expand others. This infusion of capital brought with it a different focus and intent. "The German model, which emphasized self-directed, specialized....scholarship....here there would be total intellectual freedom from....doctrinal directives," was viewed as superior to the traditional, inherited British model, the liberal arts model, which was based on the classics and focused on personal morality, philosophical consistency, theological depth, civic duty, and individual integrity.[14] "Prominent businessmen replaced ministers and denominational bureaucrats as college trustees" and "where previously orthodoxy had been the major test of an academic's eligibility for a college position, the emphasis was now almost solely on the academic's [secular] competence and credentials."[15]

Johns Hopkins University, founded in 1876, was one of the first to be based on the German model. Its focus was on science and research, expanding graduate programs, and offering professional studies in medicine and engineering, rather than focusing on religion and morality or logic and rhetoric. American education as a whole, through the course of the latter part of the nineteenth century and the entire twentieth century, became much more utilitarian than religious, much more focused on economic and social needs than on philosophy and the study of ethics.[16]

Charles Eliot, president of Harvard in 1869, is perhaps the best example of this shift in educational philosophy. He instituted the elective system to replace the classical curriculum. He emphasized the utility of the sciences and cared more for professional credentials than Christian character in his faculty. The most vigorous state universities adopted this same model, and the next generation of educators continued the promotion of the secular over the sacred and the material over the moral.[17] By

1908 it was possible to delineate the "standard American university." It was philosophically and pedagogically committed to objective, naturalistic inquiry detached from any denominational or religious restraints.

As the Church saw culture and the universities shifting toward scientism and modernism, abandoning morality and religion, it wanted nothing to do with this movement. Virtually every one of the Council for Christian Colleges and Universities (CCCU) schools was founded as a reaction to the secularization of America's universities.

BOUNDARIES

What American higher education lost when it became secularized was a necessary sense of moral boundaries—these are the boundaries of God-given truth that confirm common sense, natural law, and intellectual sanity.

A good education, a classic liberal education, is open to engaging all ideas, but with truth judging the debate—not you, me, or self-absorbed snowflakes. It is the Left's refusal to debate—its insistence on a secular, divisive, cultural Marxist orthodoxy of race, sex, and class, rather than the unifying orthodoxy of Christian truth—that is the dominant reality on campuses across the country. From violent attacks at UC Berkeley to prevent a self-styled conservative and Jewish-Catholic homosexual Milo Yiannopoulos from making his case, to Jewish conservative Ben Shapiro being prevented from speaking at DePaul University, to conservative students being arrested for handing out pocket Constitutions, the list goes on and on, and it only continues to get worse as students and administrators try to prevent themselves from having their secular, leftist, often anti-American orthodoxies challenged.[18] At most universities, intellectual nihilism, sexual licentiousness, and intolerance of dissent are the norm. At Oklahoma Wesleyan University we welcome debate within the confines, the boundaries, of a search for truth, which leads to true tolerance, respect, knowledge, civility, and intellectual development.

"When you break the big laws, you do not get liberty," said G. K. Chesterton, "you do not even get anarchy. You get the small laws." And that is what we have today on our campuses—no regulations on profanity but countless regulations on legitimate political speech; sinful invitations to sexual licentiousness and a Byzantine legal catechism to define consent; endless professions of the joys of tolerance with endless claims of microaggressions that assume everyone—or at least privileged minority groups—is expected to be rightly offended all the time. We've forgotten that education should be about perpetuating big ideas from big books and that true liberty comes when we are liberated from subjectivism by objective truth.

THE FOUR PILLARS

In our Christian faith tradition at OKWU, we identify four pillars that give students the boundaries they need to fully engage the realm of ideas: the pursuit of truth, the primacy of Christ, the priority of Scripture, and the practice of wisdom. I would argue that those four pillars position our students for optimal freedom. You don't have to share the specifics of my faith to recognize the value of these pillars:

- You are not God
- Truth exists apart from your opinion

- Truth is revealed to us, not created by us
- Where discipline thrives, freedom multiplies

On campuses all across America we see people who don't want any pillars, posts, or boundaries. They clamor for freedom, but follow what David Horowitz calls the "tyranny of the gang."

Today, universities strive to be little more than training grounds for progressive malcontents, though they would never advertise that fact so boldly. All the protests and marches are supposedly for "freedom" and "inclusivity," but when God is removed from the conversation, intrusive human government takes His place. At the end of the day, "progressive" students don't want more freedom. They want the government to redefine what is right and what is wrong, and do so with force; and it is already happening.

TIME TO GO HOME

The university was founded as a Christian institution. But most of our modern universities have denied Our Father's wisdom and ignored His teaching.

Looking at this world we have created—a world of confusion over the most basic biological truths of life and sex; of blatant dishonesty and hate disguised as tolerance and diversity; of ignorance dressed up as righteousness—perhaps it's time to ask ourselves if having our own way, outside the boundaries of the Bible, has resulted in what we expected, or if we have stumbled into a nightmare of abuse, addiction, dysfunction, irresponsibility, lies, and selfishness.

Dare we consider God is King? Dare we consider education was better in the past when we acknowledged that fact? Dare we consider America, founded in liberty under law, as given by God, is in danger of losing that freedom if we lose God? I think we should consider these questions very soberly indeed.

8

THE INTOLERANCE OF THE TOLERANT LEFT

I n *The Lion, the Witch and the Wardrobe*, Susan asks whether the great lion Aslan is "quite safe." She's told: "Who said anything about safe? 'Course he isn't safe. But he's good. He's the King...."[1]

Today in our secular culture and in academia, we've misinterpreted *safe* to mean *good*. We think it is good to say "Happy Holidays" instead of "Merry Christmas" in order to safeguard other people's ears and avoid hurting their feelings. We think safe spaces on college campuses are good because they give students an ideologically protected place to go to where nothing will be said that might offend them. We think racial segregation on college campuses keeps minority students *safe* from discrimination. We think trigger warnings are good because they provide *safety* to anyone who might be offended by a given subject or a particular idea.

But the truth is not always comfortable or safe. When Hitler's regime fell in Germany and the world saw the concentration camp horrors, the truth was very discomforting. It didn't make us feel all that safe. In fact, the images that came out of Auschwitz and Dachau were terrifying. Yet, the world needed to see this, otherwise we would never be able to confront such evil so it would never happen again.

As an educator, I'm in the business of teaching what is good and what is true, what has been tested by time, confirmed by experience, and validated by reason. As a Christian scholar I believe the best education—an education in truth as opposed to safety —is grounded in Scripture and in the timeless revelation of the self-evident truths endowed to us by our Creator; in the laws of nature and in nature's God where all true moral and intellectual training begins. "If you look for truth," said C. S. Lewis, "you may find it in the end; if you look for comfort you will get neither comfort or truth [but] only soft soap and wishful thinking to begin, and in the end, despair."[2]

Today, I find many despairing students. They cower in emotional and psychological darkness because of the nihilism of fashionable leftist ideas—in short, because of the lies of the Left. Their despair is a symptom of something even greater—something that is a grave threat to the future of American higher education and to our country as a whole.

The anti-Christian Left is intent on propagating falsehood and inverting truth. Let me give you two examples that each in its own way stands as a significant warning about the path our culture and higher education are taking.

The University of Utah announced it would award an honorary degree during its 2016 commencement ceremonies to philanthropist Lynette Nielsen Gay. Gay is the founder of Engage

Now Africa and of the Ensign College of Public Health in Kpong, Ghana. Her impressive biography includes leadership roles in organizations such as Choice Humanitarian, Southern Virginia University, Family Watch International, and the World Congress of Families (WCF).

After making its announcement, however, the university chose to edit Dr. Gay's resume on its website to expunge any references to the World Congress of Families.[3] Why? Two of the nation's most well-funded pro-LGBTQ advocacy groups—the Southern Poverty Law Center (SPLC) and the Human Rights Campaign (HRC)—had labeled WCF a "hate group" because it promotes the natural family as the "fundamental unit of society." The WCF believes the best thing for children is to grow up in a stable home environment with their biological mother and father. This is not only true on its face, but it is a truth based in love: the love of a married husband and wife and the love they have for their child. But the Left has turned such Christian love into "hate," and our universities have lost any measure of objective truth that allows them to see this Orwellian doublespeak for what it is: pure nonsense.

Another example comes from Dr. Jordan Peterson of the University of Toronto. Dr. Peterson studies the psychology of belief and did a comparative analysis of belief systems taught in schools, examining what was taught in state schools in Nazi Germany, the Soviet Union, and China, and what is taught in state schools today. He wanted to understand what would cause a large group of people to commit atrocities in service of their beliefs. He created a course called "Maps of Learning," and in that course he showed why every student in his class would have been a complicit Nazi had they lived in Germany in the 1930s.[4] Peterson's point was that madmen did not carry out these atrocities. They were carried out by ordinary people who chose safety promised to them by some very evil men at the expense of what they intuitively knew to be good and right and just.

Peterson has said many of today's college campus controversies remind him of the totalitarian regimes he studied. He has refused, for instance, to use new pronoun labels for new gender categories and now faces the prospect of criminal charges in Canada because of it. "Part of the reason I got embroiled in this gender identity controversy," he explains, "was because of what I know about how things went wrong in the Soviet Union. Many of the doctrines that underlay the legislation I've been objecting to share cultural similarities with Marxist ideas that drove Soviet communism. The thing I object to most was the insistence that people use these made up words like 'xe' and 'xer' that are the construction of authoritarians. There isn't a hope in hell that I'm going to use their language, because I know where it leads."[5]

All this is done in the name of "tolerance," but tolerance is not the same as truth and it is not synonymous with love. Frankly, as formulated by the Left on our college campuses across the land, tolerance is not even tolerant but instead, it is a tool of totalitarian *intolerance*, which denies any diversity of opinion, diversity of thought, or any final standard of truth in order to measure what is tolerable.

THE PATH OF "TOLERANCE"

Today, evangelical Christians, Catholics, and other conservative students are routinely subjected to programs on campuses that amount to little less than overt intolerance and intellectual persecution. For example, recently at the University of Pennsylvania, Cornell University, and Dartmouth College, campus activists stole and burned conservative student newspapers without facing any significant penalty from administrators. The ideas expressed in these newspapers and by these students were obviously unwelcome by the thieves in question, but they also were, apparently, not deemed worthy of toleration by the schools' presidents, provosts, and deans.

At Purdue, Vanderbilt, and Syracuse, as well as smaller universities like Castleton in Vermont, many Christian campus organizations cannot operate without violating expansive "non-discrimination" policies. Administrators at many colleges now require all student organizations to draft constitutions that pledge not to discriminate on the basis of sexual morality.[6] All lifestyles and worldviews are acceptable *except* those of orthodox Catholics, Evangelicals, and other conservatives who want to live their lives in a manner consistent with the biblical standards of sexual fidelity and the traditional morality prescribed in Scripture. Such missional clarity is simply not tolerable in these bastions of tolerance.

I SPOKE TO A "HATE GROUP"

A couple years ago, I had the privilege of being the closing keynote speaker at the World Congress of Families—an assembly that, as I have mentioned above, was labeled a "hate group" by the SPLC and the HRC. This conference brought together approximately 3,300 people of different faiths from around the world to support something very simple. As I have said, the WCF believes it is a good idea for one man and one woman to be committed to one another in marriage as they raise their children.

Put simply, the WCF believes in the family. It believes in the word *marriage* as it has been defined throughout human history.

It believes our sons and daughters do best when they have confidence their mothers and fathers are committed to each other and to them. It believes children are happier, people are healthier, and countries are freer, when a dad and a mom raise their own kids. And for championing this idea, the WCF has been branded a hate group.

The Southern Poverty Law Center condemns the World Congress of Families for its belief in—shocking as it sounds—the "natural family." The progressive/liberal Human Rights Campaign (HRC) follows suit by condemning the WCF for "exporting hate." The pro-LGBTQ periodical *The Advocate* chimes in by condemning the World Congress of Families for its pro-family agenda. It is completely unacceptable, according to *The Advocate*, to even suggest that it is best for children to have a married mom and dad raising them. This terrible idea of promoting the virtues of the nuclear family is deemed as "phobic," "extreme," and "draconian," and guilty of hate-filled "propaganda."[7]

So when people ask if I've spoken to "hate groups," I've learned how to respond. I say, Yes! I did speak to a "hate group." In fact, I've spoken to several, but the World Congress of Families was not among them. The groups that are in fact the most blatantly hateful are organizations like the SPLC, the HRC, and *The Advocate*. These are the true "hate groups." It is to them I am speaking when I condemn intolerance, bigotry, ideological fascism, injustice, and hate. It is certainly not the good Catholics, Evangelicals, and orthodox Christians who attend a conference extolling the virtues of the traditional family.

But hate is nothing to fear for Christians and other conservatives like myself. In fact, we should expect it. The followers of Christ will always be hated. We are told: "If you were the world, the world would love you as its own; but because you are not of the world, but I chose you out of the world, therefore the world hates you" (John 15:19). The early Church grew stronger in the face of hate. So too can the modern Left's opposition to the truth strengthen our Christian colleges and universities if we remain loyal to Christ and stand as witnesses to the truth, regardless of name-calling or persecution.

I believe we are living in an unprecedented time here in America. We are a nation once founded upon self-evident truth, yet are now rejecting it. Intolerance against Christians is shaping our culture—from our schools, where prayer is prohibited, to our places of work, where florists and photographers, among others, can be put out of business for refusing to compromise their moral beliefs. Even fame or celebrity is no protection. Just ask the Benham Brothers, whose HGTV show was cancelled because of their Christian beliefs on marriage and abortion.

The persecution, of course, is being done in the name of "tolerance." But as we've seen on college campuses, this is a lie. The fact is the "safe spaces" and "trigger warnings" of our universities were invented for the sole purpose of supporting intolerance. The idea that a student could escape to a "safe space" in order to avoid hearing (dare I suggest, tolerating?) something he or she finds offensive would have been unimaginable in my college days.

"Trigger warnings," the idea that college students today can claim they were emotionally wounded from language and ideas that offended them, would have been laughable even two decades ago.

Even if you are not in the world of academia, you have no doubt heard the stories of students being given failing grades simply because their beliefs were not "tolerated" by their professor. Teachers are fired or denied tenure because their beliefs are not "tolerated" by the institution employing them. Instead of teaching truth, we cater to the emotional whims of our fragile students, who are being used as pawns by cultural progressives, i.e. ideological fascists, who have found a convenient way to ban and punish conservative and Christian ideas they hate.

The First Amendment protects our freedom of speech, freedom of the press, the right to practice religion, to peacefully assemble, and the right to petition the government. This is true tolerance as defined by our founding documents. This is the right of all American citizens. Does the right of free speech end on college campuses of higher learning? Does it end when you step into a designated "safe space" at your local university? Does it end if your choice of words is construed to be a "trigger warning" when you walk into a classroom?

The answer obviously should be no. Unfortunately, the answer today on most college campuses is yes. And take this warning seriously: it won't end there.

The commentator Andrew Sullivan has noted the student anti-free-speech movement "manifests itself…almost as a religion." He continues:

> It posits a classic orthodoxy through which all of human experience is explained—and through which all speech must be filtered. Its version of original sin is the power of some identity groups over others. To overcome this sin, you need first to confess, i.e., "check your privilege," and subsequently live your life and order your thoughts in a way that keeps this sin at bay. The sin goes so deep into your psyche, especially if you are white or male or straight, that a profound conversion is required.

It operates as a religion in one other critical dimension: If you happen to see the world in a different way, if you're a liberal or libertarian or even, gasp, a conservative, if you believe that a university is a place where any idea, however loathsome, can be debated and refuted, you are not just wrong, you are immoral.... your heresy is a direct threat to others, and therefore needs to be extinguished. You can't reason with heresy. You have to ban it.[8]

Ironically, Christians, and others committed to the free expression of ideas, are the ones who are often accused of trying to force our beliefs on others. But that's not the case. Because we believe in objective truth, we believe reason and a robust exchange of ideas, with good, healthy debate can guide us to the truth. It is the radical Left that denies objective truth and therefore always relies on forced compliance and fascist tactics.

A MEASURING ROD OUTSIDE

A handful of years ago I was invited to fly to Hollywood to be part of a panel to critique the premiere of the film, *Lord, Save Us from Your Followers*. Other panelists included Michael Levine, founder and president of Levine Communications, William Lobdell, former *Los Angeles Times* religion reporter and author of *Losing My Religion*, and the film's producer, Emmy award winner Dan Merchant. I was the odd man out on the panel: a token conservative from Oklahoma to sit in juxtaposition to the smarter and more enlightened folks of Tinseltown.

The nature of Merchant's movie was simple. It was a "man-on-the-street" exposé portraying orthodox Christianity as ill-informed and intolerant; an unsophisticated belief system that is a threat to pluralism and civil discourse. Christians, it implied, should say nothing in the public square other than, "We're sorry for being so judgmental."

After the movie, we panelists took the stage. The moderator asked me the first question: "Dr. Piper, what did you think of the movie?" My response caught him and the rest of the panel off guard. I said that while I had to admit I was saddened by the thoughtless, angry people featured in the movie, I also found myself strangely amused by the obvious: the indignation this documentary sought to kindle had no meaning if there was no objective measuring rod of righteousness to contextualize the offense. In other words, in order for the movie to mock Christian moralists it had to rely on the objective standard of Christian morality to do so.

Think about it. Because Christianity is grounded in an immutable standard of rightness and wrongness—an absolute moral compass, if you will—it has the unique ability to be self-critical and self-correcting and to repent, reform, revive, and return to the right standard that Merchant, and others, are bemoaning has been compromised. Without orthodoxy (right ideas) there is no way to criticize others for lacking orthopraxy (right behavior).

C. S. Lewis, prescient as always, explained in "The Poison of Subjectivism":

> Until modern times no thinker of the first rank ever doubted that our judgments of value were rational judgments or that what they discovered was objective. It was taken for granted that in temptation passion was opposed, not to some sentiment, but to reason.

Thus Plato thought, thus Aristotle, thus Hooker, Butler and Doctor Johnson.

The modern view is very different. It does not believe that value judgments are really judgments at all. They are sentiments, or complexes, or attitudes, produced in a community by the pressure of its environment and its traditions, and differing from one community to another. To say that a thing is good is merely to express our feeling about it; and our feeling about it is the feeling we have been socially conditioned to have.

But if this is so, then we might have been conditioned to feel otherwise. "Perhaps," thinks the reformer or the educational expert, "it would be better if we were. Let us improve our morality." Out of this apparently innocent idea comes the disease that will certainly end our species (and, in my view, damn our souls) if it is not crushed; the fatal superstition that men can create values, that a community can choose its "ideology" as men choose their clothes.[9]

In my own field of education, the glorious tradition of a classical, liberal education, where men pursue truth, has been turned into something akin to the celebration of "fatal superstition" where we choose our values and governing ideologies on any given day in the same manner that "men choose their clothes."

Any schoolboy can see that the premise posed by progressives is really not about tolerance. It never has been. On the contrary, these self-styled advocates of "openness and peace" are really more interested in tyranny and power. At every turn we see them on our campuses, in our courts, and in our culture, masked in angry red faces, as they shout, "You must agree with us! You must celebrate everything we do! You must believe everything we believe! You must watch and you must applaud!" Tolerating anything they find intolerable is of no interest to them.

The end goal for these postmodern pedagogues isn't tolerance or freedom, but fascism, pure and simple. No dissent, no differences, and no diversity is allowed! It is the rule of the gang. Unquestioned and unchallenged power is their clear goal and their only rule. That's the conformity being pushed on our college campuses. That is the totalitarian conformity they have in mind for our country.

9

DO WE REALLY TRUST OURSELVES?

Prior to moving to Oklahoma, I served as the dean of students at a liberal arts college in Michigan. In my role as dean, I also taught a few classes. One of these classes was the obligatory freshman orientation course. Each year, I sought to orient my new students to life at a liberal arts institution and to challenge them to wrestle with what it meant to be a disciplined thinker. In this context, I required my students to watch the movie *Schindler's List* and then write a three-page paper. My intent was to force the students to think about the "Christian culture" of World War II Germany and ask themselves these questions: Why would any group of people ever succumb to the atrocities of the Holocaust? Why did the German culture—the culture out of which the Protestant Reformation came—lose sight of the truth to the extent that it could no longer recognize something like genocide and mass murder as being so clearly evil and wrong?

After watching this movie, one of my students (I'll call her Cynthia) turned in a paper that was fairly well written. Cynthia had obviously paid attention and engaged with the film. Her report of the movie was quite thorough. But it was the concluding sentence that I will never forget. Incredible as it seems, after watching this heart-wrenching movie and summarizing its plot, historical accuracy, and detail, Cynthia wrote: "Who am I to judge the Germans?"

For years, I and most of my peers in higher education, assumed that William Perry's theory of intellectual and ethical development was essentially an empirical fact. I studied this theory in great detail and wrote on it extensively in my graduate program at Bowling Green State University. I accepted its claims that today's students come to college with dualistic and foreclosed minds where everything is black and white, right or wrong. These students enter college with moral judgments and conclusions based on "authority." If the pastor said it was true, it's true. If mom said it was right, it's right. If dad said it was wrong, it's wrong. Accordingly, we in the ivory tower believed it was our obligation to challenge these students to grow beyond their truncated and simplistic moral assumptions grounded in rules and authority, and instead, embrace the multiple and various facets of "truth." Surely our young people needed to step away from the comforts of home and church and become more nuanced and "mature" in their morality and in their thinking.

I no longer believe this. In his book *Generation X Goes to College*, Peter Sacks contends that one of the basic characteristics of modern college students (and perhaps our culture as a whole) is the pervasive and oxymoronic belief in absolute relativism; the contention that it's all about personal choice and individual prefer-ence; the near universal judgment that it's best not to judge. Edu-cation is extremely limited if we can't get beyond subjective opinions. And subjective opinions—moral relativism—is where most students seem to want their education to begin and end, and most colleges and universities are inclined to go along. One of the problems with that approach is that our students, like Cynthia, do not have the intellectual training and moral confidence to recognize and confirm that the Holocaust, for instance, was evil not just in the minds of those who disagreed with it; it was explic-itly, absolutely evil because it violated an immutable and transcen-dent moral standard. What Cynthia needed to understand was this: we do have the right to judge the Germans. It was wrong to shoot Jews in the head and burn them in furnaces.

WHATEVER HAPPENED TO SIN?

Our culture by and large has discarded the idea of original sin. George Barna, in his book *What Americans Believe*, points out that 87 percent of non-Christians and 77 percent of self-described born again Christians agreed with the statement "Peo-ple are basically good."

The sophisticated and educated among us roll their eyes at the concept of innate human corruption. They snicker at the notion that certain actions, thoughts, and behaviors are still deemed to be sinful. The very concept of sin seems a bit too Victorian to us. It is judgmental and prudish. We are quick to condemn anyone who dares suggest that we are anything less than good people. These puritanical concepts of sin and immo-rality are, frankly, silly and simply more evidence of the intoler-ance of the Church and of conservative Christianity.

Whatever became of sin? Well, it went the way of the horse and buggy. It is an outdated and useless concept and has been replaced by more modern ways of understanding the human being and human experience. Men and women are born good and suggesting that anyone comes into this world with a corrupted nature and is guilty of sin is, well, a sin.

Because of their denial of sin, the current generation of students has lost the ability to determine whether something is right or wrong and I would argue it's frighteningly similar to the situation found in Nazi Germany, or any number of other totalitarian, fascist, or communist regimes. When people lose their ability to discern evil from good, they believe whatever they're told to believe by whoever has the most power.

The irony of this denial of the Christian understanding of human nature is that if you boil our post-modern era down to its basic premise it is really nothing more than the *celebration* of the original sin—"we shall be as God." We know all things. We define everything. Right and wrong. Good and evil. Tolerance and intolerance. Justice and injustice. What's true and what's false. Who is male and who is female. We even presume to define life and death.

Because we have declared ourselves to be "as God" we don't need Him to tell us anything any longer. Postmodernists revel in "whateverism" because everything is left up to us. We are the final measure of all things. We strut with confidence to the pulpit or to the podium and shout: *It doesn't matter what you believe as long as it works for you.* Whatever works for you! Surely it can't be wrong or sinful if it works for you, can it? This is nothing short of unmitigated moral nihilism, i.e. moral "nothingism." Such narcissism, by definition, makes the "self" the ultimate judge and final arbiter.

This all means we have indeed found a god—and it is us! As St. Paul told us in his letter to the Romans, when we exchange the truth of God for a lie we are given over to a reprobate mind and we start to worship the created rather than the creator. And what's the ultimate pinnacle of God's creation? We are! The *imago Dei*! Yes, we are the image of God, but we must not mistake that image for God. History has shown us over and over again that when men make this mistake the consequences are dire. Millions have suffered in the prisons and died in the furnaces of such idols.

Many Christians at our universities may say, "We believe in the doctrine of original sin. We believe in confession and repentance. We believe that people need to be saved and that Jesus died for our sins." But what are they teaching in their classrooms and preaching in their chapels? Are faculty confronting their students because they believe in human depravity and, as G. K. Chesterton famously argued, the most provable aspect of all of Christian theology is that people are "bad"? Or are our professors coddling our kids and telling our little darlings they are "good"? Do they treat our sons and daughters like saints or do they challenge them because they are sinners? Do they issue trigger warnings before alter calls for fear of actually making someone feel bad, or do they call *sin* by its rightful name because they know no one—no one—is truly good and even our precious little princes and princesses—our little snowflakes, like all of us, are broken and irredeemable without Christ?

Those who demand safe spaces on today's campuses betray themselves by thinking people are essentially good. Thus, they show they're really more interested in preserving someone's perception of safety than in confronting their sin. These professors and college presidents prove repeatedly that they are more satisfied with our sons' and daughters' moral and intellectual stagnation than they are committed to their growth.

Safety is synonymous with comfort, and comfort is antithetical to confrontation and growth. I have never grown in my life without being disciplined, confronted, or challenged. I have never matured and become better at much of anything, unless I was first made to feel dissonance and discomfort. Safe spaces will encourage students to do nothing more than what they already do and become nothing more than what they already are. If each of us is "good" enough, then feeling safe in that goodness may be fine. But, if we are hell-bent in our sin, then true love and good education calls for someone to stand in our way and say, "This may make you feel threatened and unsafe, but you're not as good as you think you are. Life isn't about you. You need to stop your bad behavior and think about others more than yourself!"

The irony is that, while today's students are quick to deny the reality of sin, at the same time they are crying to be protected from ideas and actions they see as "sinful"—things they don't want to hear; things they don't want to see or experience; things and people they believe to be wrong. This new world of "safe spaces" is very much an "us" versus "them" paradigm. Consequently, because today's post-mods and millennials see themselves as sinless, anyone who dares disagree with them is sinful. In an effort to protect themselves from anyone and any idea they disagree with, their call for "safety" has become a tool of emotional and ideological fascism.

They create a campus "collective" bound in unbroken compliance and agreement. If you're part of their tribe, you are good and welcomed. But, if you break rank and refuse to embrace the acceptable ideas, you are bad. You're no longer deemed "safe" and you need to be silenced or removed. You'll be fired from your position or your enrollment will be terminated. You must submit. You must confess. You must convert. While ridiculing the allegedly antiquated concept of sin, they brand you a sinner.

Those who are bound to this ideological fascism may feel safe, but being "safe" does not mean being good. The Nazis following Hitler were "safe," but they weren't good. There's a reason why prisons are called "maximum *security*." The prisoner enjoys great safety, but he has no freedom. The gang feels safe as long as it has power, but heaven help the poor soul who wants to break ranks with the gang.

In any form of collectivism, members eventually turn on each other. If the people in the "safe space" don't believe in right or wrong, the evil they bring with them will result in them doing whatever they want to each other without judgment because they couldn't possibly ever be wrong. Thus, the Occupy Wall Street movement was replete with stories of physical violence, rapes, and public defecating within the "safe space" of the very people protesting alleged oppression. It wasn't safe. It was anarchy.

People sincerely searching for the truth may think they can find it by creating "safe spaces," through being politically correct, or through forced "tolerance," but at the end of the day, all of these tactics only create a vacuum in culture to be filled by something else. Elementary physics teaches us that vacuums will always be filled by something. When you take God out of the public square it creates a vacuum quickly filled with garbage. The vacuum is readily filled by those lusting for power, and the result is more and more laws to control fallen human beings, no matter how stridently we deny our brokenness.

As Billy Preston, that great pop "philosopher" of the 1970s told using his song, "Nothing from Nothing,"[1] sooner or later, nothing is always filled with something as people seek to make sense out of nonsense. The vacuum is always filled with either God's principles or man's power, and when we disparage and discard the immutable laws of nature and nature's God, power *always* rushes in to fill the void.

This is a proven pattern in human history. The story of every despot and totalitarian leader proves this point. We need look no further than the examples of Pol Pot, Mao, Stalin, and Robespierre. Do you think all those who starved in the Gulag under Stalin felt safe? What about the two million people in the killing fields of Pol Pot? What about those who waited at the gallows of Robespierre, a man who declared himself to be as god and used the guillotine to silence all who dared challenge his alleged goodness? Vacuums are always filled and the hubris of mankind will always seek to find a "hero" to fill the "zero" created by denying the sacred in our quest for safety.

These and hundreds of other examples demonstrate that it is a monumental mistake to build governments and to construct a culture on the premise that people are essentially good. We are all broken and prone to think of ourselves as gods. Until recently, we taught students to acknowledge that brokenness and pursue God's truth in order to protect the world from them; to guard against the evil that lurks in every human heart. Now we teach them that they are the saviors of their own souls while insisting there is no such thing as sin.

WHO AM I TO JUDGE?

"The Lottery" is a classic, though disturbing, short story written by Shirley Jackson in 1948. It's the tale of a rural, farming community in America of about three hundred residents. The town seems normal by all accounts as it prepares for a traditional, harvest-time event known as The Lottery. Each year the name of every family is written on a piece of paper and securely stored in a locked box. On the morning of the annual gathering, the heads of each household draw from the box until a paper slip with a black spot is extracted.

Upon "winning" this phase of the lottery, each member of the Hutchinson family then draws slips of paper out of another box until one member of the family—the mother, named Tessie—draws a piece of paper with the final black spot on it. In spite of her cries, the townspeople, including her own husband and children, stone her to death to ensure a more prosperous harvest.[2]

The story has rightly been included in literary anthologies for its shocking portrayal of the power of groupthink and the human inclination to accept evil. For more than thirty years beginning in 1970, English professor Kay Haugaard used the story to spark discussions of morality in her literature class. Dr. Haugaard says she could always count on some common reactions:

> Everyone thought it was scary because, as someone inevitably said, "The characters seem just like regular people—you know, like us!"
>
> The story always impressed the class with the insight that I felt the author had intended: the danger of just "going along" with something habitually, without examining its rationale and value.... In spite of the changes that I had witnessed over the years in anthologies and in students' writing, Jackson's message about blind conformity always spoke to my students' sense of right and wrong.[3]

Then in the 1990s something started to change dramatically in how her students responded to the sobering tale. Rather than being horrified by it, some claimed they were bored by it, while others thought the ending was "neat." When she pressed them for more of their thoughts, she was appalled to discover that not one student in the class was willing to say the practice of human sacrifice was morally wrong! She describes one interaction with a student, whom she calls Beth, in *The Chronicle of Higher Education*:

> "Are you asking me if I believe in human sacrifice?" Beth responded thoughtfully, as though seriously considering all aspects of the question.
>
> "Well, yes," I managed to say. "Do you think that the author approved or disapproved of this ritual?" I was stunned: This was the [young] woman who wrote so passionately of saving the whales, of concern for the rain forests, of her rescue and tender care of a stray dog.
>
> "I really don't know. If it was a religion of long standing..."
>
> For a moment I couldn't even respond. This woman actually couldn't seem to bring herself to say plainly that she was against human sacrifice. My classes of a few years before would have burst into nervous giggles at the suggestion. This class was calmly considering it.[4]

At one point a student explained she had been taught not to judge and if this practice worked for them, who was she to argue differently. Appalled by the student's moral indifference, Haugaard concludes, "Today, for the first time in my thirty years of teaching, I looked my students in the eye and not one of them in my class could tell me that this society, this cultural behavior was a bad thing."[5]

What have we done? Not one of these students would say human sacrifice is wrong? The whole point of "The Lottery" is to show the dangers of blindly following such dangerous ideas. But, these students had been taught that labels like *good* and *evil*, *sacred* and *sinful*, no longer applied as absolutes—and they responded accordingly. They had been taught that to assign moral values to actions was, in itself, wrong. God help us!

Remember the false encouragement of the *Polar Express* conductor: "It doesn't matter where [you're] going. What matters is deciding to get on." Can we really trust ourselves—or the next generation—to "get on" the right train? Why should we be surprised when they calmly and coldly declare, "It doesn't matter what you believe as long as it works for you. The whole idea of sin is silly. If it works for them, who are we to judge?"

10

OUR CULTURAL AVERSION TO ADVERSITY

A puzzling case was once brought before a king. Two women presented their problem to Solomon, known as the wisest judge on earth. There was plenty of finger pointing, anger, and tearful accusations. At dispute was a baby—both women claimed to be the mother. Both pleaded desperately for the baby. Both claimed the other was lying.

Solomon's simple solution was both shocking and bold. He ordered his bodyguard to cut the baby in two and give half to each woman. Upon hearing the king's judgment, the real mother cried out, "Don't kill him! Give him to the other woman." Her instinctive behavior revealed the truth, for no mother would let her son be cut in two.

I think of this story often as I look at the present state of the academy within our contemporary culture. There was a time not long ago when it was assumed an educated person was one who understood the interconnectedness of all aspects of our existence. One discipline informed the other. Religion and science were interrelated. The humanities were built upon philosophy and vice versa. Economics informed ethics and ethics informed economics.

This was a time when division played no role in education. Instead, there was harmony between music and math. Faith and learning were intertwined. The university stood for "unity." Professors, preachers, and politicians all knew a healthy culture was one built upon an integrated body of knowledge, not a segregated collection of disaffected opinions. Truth stood the test of time and withstood the corruption of power. It was self-evident that we can't separate faith from facts or belief from behaviors, for both presuppose the other.

Today, however, our post-modern universities seem adrift in self-refuting and disconnected claims that fly in the face of logic. Tolerance is championed by faculty who won't tolerate those they judge to be intolerant. Diversity is claimed as the highest good by students who openly detest those with whom they disagree. Academic freedom is demanded by the same people who employ political correctness to restrict public debate.

The same sort of academicians who railed against government intrusion during the Scopes Monkey Trial now lobby for a government-imposed curriculum that prohibits an open exchange of ideas concerning human origins and Intelligent Design. Many scholars now declare that one's personal life is off limits when assessing a person's fitness for public service. The "content of a man's character" is no longer as important as the color of his skin or his other physical characteristics and political loyalties.

Is it possible that in the story of Solomon we find a timely and poignant lesson for today? The question is this: Are we more like the woman who was willing to let the king cut the baby in half than we are like the one who cried out to save her child? As we see post-modern fallacies sawing our culture asunder, separating public policy from personal piety, are we willing to let the king "cut the baby in half" or do we plead for him to save the child even if it hurts us to do so?

As we see our schools, our churches, and our media constructing false dichotomies that sever our children's personal beliefs from their public behavior, their facts from their faith, and their heads from their hearts, do we tacitly let the king carry out his gruesome work or do we shout, stop!

When we see the consequences of our broken ideas paraded before us on the evening news in Columbine-like vignettes, do we cry out, *No, I won't let you continue to cut the soul out of my son or daughter. He needs morality to be a man. She needs piety to have purpose. Take your sword away and let my child live*!

Solomon knew a living thing could not be cut in half and expected to survive. C. S. Lewis's words of a half-century ago call us to heed the same lessons of this wisest man in history: "We have made such a tragic comedy of the situation—We continue to clamor for those very qualities we are rendering impossible. You can hardly open a periodical without coming across the statement that what our civilization needs is more self-sacrifice, [honesty], and [ethics]. In a sort of ghastly simplicity we [have removed] the organ [while we continue to] demand the function. We make men without chests and expect of them virtue.... We laugh at honor and are shocked to find traitors in our midst. We castrate and bid the geldings to be fruitful." Scripture tells us "Faith without works is dead"(James 2:17). Perhaps the lesson of Solomon is that a culture emasculated of its character is dead too.

GOD, GIVE US HEROES

What are the consequences of rearing a generation of moral amputees—a nation of characterless children who dodge every difficulty and run from every conflict and challenge as well as every pain and sorrow? We have taught tomorrow's leaders to avoid if not blatantly deny life's hard truths. Rather than facing adversity with courage, our nation's next generation of congressmen, senators, CEOs, and presidents now cower in campus counseling centers complete with Play-Doh, bubbles, puzzles, and coloring books. Why are we surprised at their lack of ability to deal with reality? When we coddle our kids we may mean well, but the result is a culture of perpetual adolescents who are crippled morally and intellectually and, thus, incapable of wrestling with the inevitable adversities in life.

Where would America and the rest of the world be if it had always been this way; if we had not had brave young men and women who ran toward danger instead of cowering and demanding safe spaces? Rev. George W. Rutler, pastor of St. Michael's Church in New York City, recognizes the cultural impact of our pampering:

> The average age of a Continental soldier in the American Revolution was one year less than that of a college freshman today. Alexander Hamilton was a fighting lieutenant-colonel when 21, not to mention Joan of Arc who led an army into battle and saved France when she was about as old as an American college sophomore. In our Civil War, eight Union generals and seven Confederate generals were under the age of 25. The age of most U.S. and RAF fighter pilots in World War II was about that of those on

college junior varsity teams. Catholics who hoped in
this election for another Lepanto miracle will remember that back in 1571, Don Juan of Austria saved
Western civilization as commanding admiral when he
was 24. None of these figures, in the various struggles
against the world and the flesh and devil, retreated to
safe spaces weeping in the arms of grief therapists.[1]

The real world has always demanded young men and women
to step up, often before they thought themselves ready to face
reality. Our "Greatest Generation" did so for ideals that tran-
scended themselves and their own desires. But our young people
today seem to be intent on satiating their every appetite and
satisfying their every whim and inclination. Anything that keeps
them from fulfilling their desires is deemed oppressive. On college campuses all across America, we're teaching students that
one's proclivities always take precedent over principles, and that
comfort always trumps self-control and courage. That cannot
bode well for the fate of our nation, because freedom isn't free.

To bring this cultural warning to life, I turn again to C. S.
Lewis and his enchanted tales from the Chronicles of Narnia. In
The Silver Chair, the fifth book in the series, we find three main
characters: two children named Scrubb and Jill, and a Narnian
friend called Puddleglum. Aslan the mighty lion instructs these
three adventurers to venture into a dark underground world in
search of Rilian, the Prince of Narnia, who has been kidnapped
by an evil witch.

They find the prince in a dark and dank cavern underground,
tied to a silver chair that has mysterious powers over him. He
has been brainwashed to believe the witch is his ally, not his
captor, that darkness is light, and that his bondage is freedom.

The kids and Puddleglum untie the prince, hoping to escape the confines of the cave before the witch returns. But, alas, they are too late. The witch returns and captures them before they can flee the darkness of the Underworld and return to the warm sun-drenched lands of Narnia.

Standing before the witch in the cave barely lit by smoldering smudge pots Jill, Scrubb, and Puddleglum confront their captor. They demand she let them return home. They want to see the sun and feel its warm rays. They want to run in the cool of the evening, bathe in moonbeams, lie in the grass, and count the stars. They want to escape from the ugly world of the witch's making and return instead to Narnia. They want to experience what is right and true, to be free again with Aslan.

The witch doesn't resort to force to try to keep them enslaved. Instead, she chooses to use the power of words and ideas to question the very nature of reality:

> "What is this sun that you all speak of?" [asked the witch] Do you mean anything by the word? ... Can you tell me what it's like?"
>
> "Please it your Grace," said the prince. "You see that lamp. It is round and yellow and gives light to the whole room; and hangeth moreover from the roof. Now that thing which we call the sun is like the lamp, only far greater and brighter. It giveth light to the whole Overworld and hangeth in the sky."
>
> "Hangeth from what, my lord?" Asked the witch and then, while they were all still thinking how to answer her, she added, with another of her soft, silver laughs, "You see? When you try to think out clearly what this sun must be, you cannot tell me. You can

only tell me it is like the lamp. Your sun is a dream and there is nothing in that dream that was not copied from the lamp. The lamp is the real thing; the sun is but a tale and children's story."[2]

Doesn't the witch's reality-bending argument sound familiar? Over my twenty years of working within the academy, I have found today's campuses to be as dark, dank, and fake as the witch's Underworld. The materialist says there is no truth beyond what you can touch, feel, taste, and see. As Carl Sagan declares, "The Cosmos is all there ever was and ever will be."[3] The post-modernist says there is no truth at all. Foucault, Rorty, Lyotard, and a host of others all join with the witch to declare there are no suns, only lamps. Dreams of lions are merely religion's wishful hopes of what cats could be. There are no immutable standards. There really is no such thing as good and evil—no universal truths, no Narnia, no Overworld, no sky, no sun, no Aslan.

"You have seen lamps," said the witch, "and so you imagined a bigger and better lamp and called it the sun. You've seen cats, and now you want a bigger and better cat, and it's to be called a lion." Sorcerers of a different sort on campuses make similar spellbinding arguments. You talk of the *imago Dei*, and I say, there is no *imago Dei*. There's nothing but the imago dog, primordial ooze, and a biological mass. You talk of the grandeur of creation and I say, *No*, there's nothing but the tactile in which you can taste and touch and see and smell. You talk of truth, goodness, and higher ideals, but I say you have only imagined and wished they were so.

Yet there is a way out of this dark cave. Freedom is found, as it was for those children, by following the path of the marsh-wiggle

Puddleglum. Even after the prince and the children had given up hope and begun to mindlessly repeat the witch's mantra, Puddleglum refused to forsake the truth. He decided to fight back.

He got as close as possible to what he knew to be real—*pain*:

> While the Prince and the two children were standing with their heads hung down, their cheeks flushed, their eyes half closed, the strength all gone from them; the [witch's] enchantment almost complete,... Puddleglum, desperately gathering all his strength, walked over to the fire [and] with his bare foot he stamped on [it]. The pain itself made [his] head for a moment perfectly clear and he knew exactly what he really thought. **There is nothing like a good shock of pain for dissolving certain kinds of magic.** [Emphasis mine]

Puddleglum broke the witch's spell of false words and ideas by forcing himself to engage with what was painful and uncomfortable, but true. The way to distinguish between what is false and what is fact is to follow Puddleglum's example. We must recognize there are some things in life that are real and hot and true. To know the difference between "suns and lamps" and "lions and cats" we must get as close to reality as we possibly can. Stepping into the fire of ideas and truth might hurt for a while, but "there is nothing like a good shock of pain for dissolving certain kinds of magic."

Only by pressing through adversity was Puddleglum able to rediscover the truth. And so it is with us. Have we sacrificed ourselves to be satisfied with the safety of the "lamp" instead of the true warmth of the "sun"? Have we sacrificed reality to live in comfort in a cultural Underworld? Have we become a bunch of navel-gazers, fixated on the inferior and assuming there's nothing more? Liberation from ideological darkness can only happen when we have the courage to pursue reality—to step right into it, pain and all—and not be satisfied with postmodern chants and constructs. We must embrace the pain necessary for truth to exist. Just as great leaders throughout history had to sacrifice comfort for pain in order to promote and protect truth, we must do the same.

The witch's Underworld is a sobering picture of being content with the fake and the inferior. So many of the dilemmas we face on campuses and across our nation right now come from people being unable to stomach reality. We've responded to this struggle by conjuring up a false reality that appears to be a "safe space." Ironically, although Christian and other private schools are often accused of placing children in a bubble, it is the secularists today who insist we all join them in their own fantasy land; an Orwellian bubble, where men can be women, sex has no consequences, and words like truth, goodness, and justice can mean whatever they want them to mean.

Adversity yields strength; bubbles produce weak people with misguided passions. So many protesters talk of "freedom," yet it is not freedom they seek, but bondage. The grand and beautiful ideas of Christianity, freedom, and justice, have been hijacked to mean control and dominance, entitlement and enslavement. It's as if they are saying, *It is delusional to think there are suns and moons and lions—freedom and justice and righteousness and dignity. There's nothing such as the human being. There's nothing such as the female. There is nothing such as the male. There's nothing such as a free society. The only reason socialism hasn't worked yet is that it hasn't been tried the right way and we're smart enough to impose it upon all of culture and make it work.*

The list of delusions goes on and on. We need to step toward, not away from, the cultural pain required to wake us up. Even though its heat may hurt and its flame may singe our consciences and burn our souls a bit, we need to get as close as we can to the "fire" of the good, the true, and the beautiful once again. Truly great schools and teachers should want to give a shocking dose of truth to every student. Good teachers should not want to make students *feel* safe, comfortable, or even good. They should call our young men and women to go higher up and higher in. They should call them to growth and maturity, to reach for the sun, not settle for the lamp.

Those things worth having in life often require persevering through pain and pressing forward through adversity to achieve. Our students need confronting, not coddling, to survive in the real world, to realize their full potential, and become the heroes of self-sacrifice we need them to be. When we shield our children from reality, we keep them from being prepared for living. As a result, when confronted by a world crisis or conflict that can't be solved with puppies and rainbows, they won't have a clue what to do. They will cave. Our military today seems more interested in naming a new ship the *Harvey Milk* to celebrate a gay activist's legacy as a pedophile than in preparing to do its job of standing in the way of bad ideas and killing bad people.[4]

OUR PATH TO THE DIVINE

In previous chapters, I exposed the myth of creating a utopian world by ignoring our brokenness and innate sinful nature. This is a worldview grounded in the false assumption that if we just give the right kind of people—the smart people—enough power, the world's problems can be avoided. This is a dangerous fantasy. It is a lie. It is a fairy tale; a make believe land built upon nothing more than mankind's arrogance and selfish pursuits, and governed by nothing but the faddish opinions of an elite club of "know-it-alls." It is an oligarchy, as it maneuvers to acquire more and more power over those it wishes to hold powerless and view as less enlightened.

Progressives frequently point fingers at those who disagree with them, calling them "racist, sexist, homophobic, or religious zealots!" Yet, without fail, they almost never have any facts or evidence to support such labels and accusations. Unfortunately, by and large we have come to accept their lies. We are no longer on a quest for truth where we apply God's revelation and natural law to the difficult areas of life. Instead we have embraced the upside-down fantasies of the Left, exchanging them for the truth. One example of this is evident in the field of science, where, yes, we surely should recognize that science is good, but at the same time we should be quick to admit that science clearly isn't God.

In a recent op-ed in *The Huffington Post*, Victor Stenger, author of *God: The Failed Hypothesis. How Science Shows That God Does Not Exist*, bemoaned America's educational decline and more specifically its loss of status in the sciences. As evidence of his concern Stenger contends, "Once America was the foremost nation in science [but today]...our schools are producing a generation of science illiterates."[5] He goes further to say many critics who write on the subject "blame American scientists for doing a poor job," but, confident in his superior intellect, Dr. Stenger quickly dismisses such a possibility of professional culpability and boldly points where he believes the fault lies. The obvious culprit for such glaring failure is religion and, more specifically, conservative Christianity.

"From its very beginning in prehistory," contends the good professor, "religion has been a tool used by those in power to retain that power and keep the masses in line [and] this continues today." He then concludes: "I have an urgent plea to...all thinking people. We need to focus our attention on one goal [that] has to be achieved...if humanity is to survive: That goal is the replacement of foolish faith and its vanities with something more sublime—knowledge and understanding that is securely based on observable reality."

I agree with Dr. Stenger's emphasis on the empirical and would like to propose some examples of how he and all other "thinking people" might consider setting aside "foolish faith," and seek, instead, the clarity of what is "observably real." For instance, it seems clear and observable that gender is a biological reality and not a human construct, and there is nothing more empirically obvious than the fact that a baby is a boy or a girl and that Bruce Jenner is a man.

It likewise seems clear and observable that certain behaviors plainly compromise the design and purpose of the human body and that any sexual act other than one between a monogamous man and monogamous woman predictably causes disease and dysfunction and should logically be avoided.

It seems clear that for at least two thousand years, Western civilization has affirmed (to its obvious advantage) the ontologically obvious definition of marriage. It is, likewise, observably clear that children do best when they have both a mom and a dad bound to one another in such a marriage. It seems clear that a mother fares better when she is married to the father of her children. It also seems clear that our efforts at social engineering have resulted in untold poverty and dysfunction for these same women and their children.

There are so many things that are clear and observable. It is clear, for example, that socialism only works until you run out of other people's money. It is clear that power corrupts and absolute power corrupts absolutely. It is clear that liberty is always lost when licentiousness abounds. It is clear that women suffer most when men are without morals.

It is clear that some absolutes cannot be tested in a tube and yet must be affirmed. For example, it is clear racism is bad, rape is wrong, and the Holocaust should have been avoided. Surely no "thinking person" such as Dr. Stenger would deny such empirical facts, even if such truths cannot be derived from the laboratory or a Petri dish? It is also clear that it takes about as much "foolish faith and vanity" to believe nature's design has no designer as it does to suppose a painting has no painter, a building has no builder, a book has no writer, or a watch has no watchmaker.

Yes, Dr. Stenger, we do "need to focus our attention on one goal." Yes, we must replace our "foolish faith and its vanities" with "something more sublime." Yes, this should be "knowledge and understanding that is securely based on observable reality." And yes, Dr. Stenger, this reality is about as clear and observable as the very nose on your own face if you would but open your eyes to see. As the prophet Jeremiah wrote, "Now hear this, O foolish and senseless people, who have eyes but do not see; who have ears but do not hear" (Jeremiah 5:21).

Chuck Colson wrote, "We all base our lives on some vision of ultimate reality that gives meaning to our individual existence. If we reject God, we will put something in his place; we will absolutize some part of creation.... Biology takes the place of

God as the ultimate reality, and sex becomes the path to the divine."[6]

Is this not true? We live in a culture where "science" has been dubbed the ultimate reality. The result at a basic level is the steady decline of morality, including the glorification of sex outside of marriage, which destroys the foundations of culture and leads to a series of consequences that follow like a line of dominos. Colson continues, "science itself has become one of the most popular forms of redemption." Science has replaced religion and the moment it does, morality is also destroyed.

Just one example of this is the rise of the utopian belief that we can act as the creator and form life ourselves through genetic engineering. The ultimate hope is to create perfect people by our own hand and through our advanced knowledge. We have turned "science into a myth of salvation." Once again, this is the slippery slope that leads sinful people to think they can and should decide who is fit and who is not. You see, science is good, but it isn't God. And when the "smart folks" start using science for things such as creating a master race, genetic engineering can quickly become eugenics and the educated and intelligent ones among us—the "brights"—come perilously close to playing God to the detriment of all who aren't deemed as smart as them. In the hands of the arrogant, science can become a dangerous thing: a tool of oppression and death rather than one of liberation and life.

As Colson said, "Bigger and better technology simply gives people bigger and better means to carry out either good or evil choices." Ideas have consequences—for cultures as well as individuals.

CULTURE OF INSTABILITY

When we never know from one year to the next what is real and what is imaginary, we end up with a culture of instability that makes our continued existence precarious at best. When we don't know from one year to the next what the word marriage might mean, we end up with unstable families producing unstable citizens. When we don't know what goodness means from one month to the next, our ethics and justice systems falter.

Who can respect the rule of law in a culture that claims there is no good or evil? How can the underdog ever plan for his future in a society where might makes right? How can businesses like Hobby Lobby make a five-year plan when they never know if they will be forced to compromise their religious beliefs? Such unpredictability increases risk and risk always increases the economic costs of doing business. Who can make plans in such an environment, even plans for good? Why would loving people start a non-profit to help the poor when they might be dragged before the Supreme Court like the Little Sisters of the Poor? When we insist on living in a fantasy of our own imagination and when we double down on ignoring reality, the whims of those in power rule the day. What one president decrees by order, the next one reverses. And so it goes.

We end up with a culture of instability in which nothing can thrive because we never know from one day to the next what is right or wrong, what is male or female, what marriage is or isn't, what is true and what is a lie, or what is just and what is unjust. In such a world all definitions are lost. Words mean nothing. Words like life, liberal, liberation, love, marriage, sex—and even words like science become nothing but "fluid constructs" and thereby carry no empirical or lasting value. It's impossible to be a real scientist and claim to "know" that anything is true and right and real in such a shifting cultural landscape.

Our present cultural preoccupation with postmodernity is actually antithetical to science. It's suicidal. And it has to stop.

11

OUR EDUCATION NIGHTMARE

Imagine we live in a day where we intentionally sever a man's arm from his body and then expect him to win a fight, where we pluck a woman's eyes from her head and then ask her to paint her own portrait, or where we surgically remove a child's frontal lobe and demand she explain an algebraic formula. Imagine we live in a world where, as C. S. Lewis warned, the elite among us actually claim it makes sense to geld the stallion and then "bid him be fruitful." Imagine we live in a time and place where the wise and learned in our courts and classrooms and churches remove a man's soul and then expect him to stay out of hell. Such a day is now upon us.

Through our broken public schools and the failed educational paradigm of the National Education Association (NEA), we continue to coddle our students via social engineering and politically correct indoctrination. We promote students from one grade level to the next, not because of any actual academic achievement but because they "participated." Then we give them a trophy (i.e. a high school diploma).

The result is a citizenry unable to read or write. According to the Nation's Report Card, only 37 percent of twelfth-graders were proficient in reading in 2015, and just 25 percent were proficient in math.[1] However, in spite of the dropping scores, graduation rates continue to rise. This means we have a generation of young people where we have "severed the organ but demand the function." We have a society with no understanding of how to multiply and divide, a workforce without the skills to work, and an electorate with no clear moral code—a truly crippled nation.

The problem in education is not a lack of money—we're spending more than ever before. The problem is not a matter of access to the "right curriculum." The problem is we have abandoned the priorities of character and moral development along with teaching logical reasoning and objective truth. We have failed to give children a foundation they can use to learn on their own. Instead, we give them a host of foundationless bad ideas. Bad ideas breed bad behavior as surely as an acorn grows an oak or a hurricane brings a flood.

Why would we expect decades of teaching sexual promiscuity in our schools to result in sexual restraint in our students? Why are we surprised at the selfishness of our culture when our schools teach self-esteem more effectively than they do mathematics, science, and civics? How can we possibly think teaching values clarification rather than moral absolutes will produce a virtuous people? Where in the annals of history is there any evidence that the subordination of one person's right to live to another person's right to choose ever resulted in the protection of every person's unalienable right to life? Why would any culture ever think that after decades of diminishing the value of marital fidelity the same culture would then be able to mount a vigorous defense for the meaning of marriage?

This list could go on, but the evidence is clear. All we need to do is turn on the nightly news to see the proof. When we separate fact from faith and head from heart, and when we sever belief from behavior or religion from reason, we do not usher in a day of liberty but one of licentiousness. We become "men without chests" where there is nothing but a gaping cavity in the center of our being—where instead of finding the fullness which comes from fidelity—we find the emptiness of a love affair gone bad.

We live in such a day and time. Our schools are stagnant with the heavy air of our own hypocrisy. We boast of freedom and yet live in bondage to our own deception. We champion civil liberties, yet we ignore the human rights promised to us by tradition, reason, Scripture, and our own Constitution. We say women should not be subjugated to the power and passions of men, but we then embrace leaders who publicly use women for their own selfish whims. We draw a line in the sand to defend the innocence of children while at the same time we enjoy "entertainment" that blurs the boundaries between our own children and predatory adults who are anything but innocent. We are indeed "people of the lie." It seems as if the road to hell is before us, and we enter its gates strutting with the confidence of an emperor with no clothes. And, when challenged, we belittle the "naïveté" of those who dare shout out our nakedness.

Pressing our ear against the keyhole of history, we hear the voices of our forefathers saying, "Liberty is given by our Creator and slavery is constructed by man." Their lessons teach us that self-evident truth is the only context for justice and freedom and that without objective standards as our rule and measure, men and women find innumerable ways to enslave themselves and each other while waving a sanctimonious banner of personal choice and individual rights.

Ideas have consequences. Education will always lead some-where—either toward the liberty found in that which is right and just and real, or toward the slavery and ugly hell made of our own dysfunction. As C. S. Lewis states, "All your life long you are slowly turning…either into a heavenly creature or into a hellish creature: either into [one who] is in harmony with God…or one that is in a state of war and hatred with God.… To be the one kind of creature is heaven: that is, it is joy and peace and knowledge and power [and liberty]. To be the other means madness…[and slavery]."[2]

WHY I AM A LIBERAL

This is why I believe, as I mentioned earlier, that today's constitutional conservative is in fact yesterday's classical liberal. Let me explain in more detail here. The world *liberal* implies liberty and liberty demands justice and freedom—in that context I am a *liberal*! The current cultural definition of liberal has been stolen, co-opted and, frankly, perverted into something it was never intended to be. Progressives know full well that by turning definitions upside down and using a vocabulary most people don't understand, they are able to get away with much more, and deceive the average person.

With this as context, I argue it is time for conservatives to reclaim the high ground of what it means to be a classical liberal.

I am a liberal because I believe the best education is one that indeed liberates. It liberates us from the consequences of those things that are wrong and frees us to live within the beauty of those things that are right.

I am a liberal because of my passion for the liberal arts—an education driven by the hunger for answers rather than the protection of opinions, an education not subject to the ebb and flow of personal agendas or political fads, an education not afraid to put all ideas on the table because there is confidence that in the end we will embrace what is true and discard what is false.

I am a liberal because I believe in freedom—freedom of thought and expression and the freedom to dissent from consensus. I am energized by the unapologetic pursuit of truth. Wherever it leads, I am confident in the words, "You shall know the truth, and the truth shall set you free" (John 8:32).

I am a liberal because I believe in integration. Truth cannot be segregated into false dichotomies, but it is an integrated whole. The liberally educated person recognizes we cannot and should not separate personal life from private life, the head from the heart, fact from faith, or belief from behavior.

I am a liberal because I believe in conservation. There are ideas tested by time, defended by reason, validated by experience, and confirmed by revelation; and these ideas should be conserved. I believe in common sense and natural law. We do know rape is wrong, the Holocaust was bad, and hatred and racism are to be reviled. Even though we cannot produce these truths in a test tube, we hold them to be self-evident laws no human being can deny.

I am a liberal because I recognize that when we exchange the truth for a lie, we build a house of cards that will fall to mankind's inevitable temper tantrum of seeking control and power.

History tells us time and time again that to deny what is right and true and embrace what is wrong and false is to fall prey to the rule of the gang or the tyranny of one.

I am a liberal because I believe in liberty. I believe liberty is the antithesis of slavery and slavery is the unavoidable outcome of lies: lies about who we are as people, lies about what is right and what is wrong, lies about man and lies about God.

Good education—complete education—*liberal* education must be grounded in the conservative respect for and the conservation of what is immutable and right and just and real. It should seek to reclaim what has been co-opted and reveal what has been compromised. It should be free of intimidation and should honor open inquiry and the right to dissent. It should have confidence in the measuring rod of truth—that unalienable standard that is bigger and better than the crowd, the consensus, or the common core.

Education—good, liberal education—is the business of pursuing truth. It is about the exceptional and not just the common. It is about character and not just a career. It is about integrity and not just information. It is about morality and not just mathematics. It is about teaching truth and not teaching to a text.

Good education isn't about dumbing down our curriculum to some banal commonality of mediocre standards constructed by nameless groups of bureaucrats from some distant town and some distant state. It isn't about legislative arrogance. It's about local control. It isn't about the State's hunger for power, it's about the student's hunger for answers. It isn't about government fiat, it's about academic freedom. Good education isn't about the president telling parents what ideas we must teach. It's about parents holding the president to constitutional constraints.

Good education isn't about the perpetuation of the common. As Martin Luther King Jr., told us in his letter from the Birmingham jail, it is the conservation of the immutable, exceptional, and God-given virtues that serve as our strongest justification for the ongoing struggle for freedom, liberation, and liberty.[3] Without such uncommon—and conservative—ideas, progressives make a mockery of intellectual liberty and academic freedom.

We see this arrogance often from modern-day liberals who, knowing that the liberal label is wearing thin, have reverted to using the tag of progressives they used a century ago. Andrew Cuomo, governor of New York, told people in 2014 that those who disagree with him can leave the state.[4] He specifically said "anyone who is pro-traditional marriage, pro-life or pro-guns—[has] no place in the state of New York." How open-minded and tolerant of him. His comments are just one more example of the ideological fascism of progressive elites. This is not intellectual liberty.

In my televised debate with the school superintendent of Stillwater public schools, I argued that common core is the antithesis of academic freedom. She concluded her statements by saying, "Common Core is the law and we aren't going to talk about it any more." She couldn't have made my point any better. The state has decided what we can talk about, so just be quiet.

Likewise, in my debate with Brian Hunt of the Tulsa School Board, I argued for local control and parental responsibility. Mr. Hunt responded by saying, "Dr. Piper, do you really believe we can trust communities like Hugo and Sallisaw with such local control of their kids' education?" What arrogance and condescension. I responded by saying, "Mr. Hunt, with all due respect, last I knew the homeschooled kids from Hugo and Sallisaw do a lot better on almost every measure of education success than the poor kids subjected to the terrible schools under your charge."

The students coming out of our current education system are creating havoc in the workforce. Many employers are refusing to hire employees from the millennial generation because they lack a decent work ethic.[5] One business owner said what I hear a lot: "I'm convinced these people [millenials] want to have jobs—they just don't want to work. It's hard to tell if they can't do the work or if they just simply don't want to." Another boss said, "There's a level of career impatience that used to be reserved for the 'kids that were too smart for their grade,' justifying misbehavior with boredom. Now the entire grade feels too smart for their grade—and we have to manage that."[6] The important skills lacking in many graduates when they go into the workforce are "critical thinking, problem solving, attention to detail, and writing proficiency."[7] Marian Salzman, CEO of Havas PR US, told CBS News, "You do have to speak to [millennials] a little bit like a therapist on television might speak to a patient. You can't be harsh. You cannot tell them you're disappointed in them. You can't really ask them to live and breathe the company. Because they're living and breathing themselves and that keeps them very busy."[8]

COMMON CORE

When I was asked to get involved in the Common Core debate, I was reluctant to do so. It's a complicated issue, and I thought I really didn't have time to figure out all the reasons why Common Core is a bad idea. However, the more I saw the sorry state of students emerging from our school systems, the more I realized it needed to be confronted. Common Core, at its core, suggests that the curriculum choices made by somebody in San Francisco, New York, or Washington, DC are superior to those made by parents and local authorities. Those curriculum choices that are imposed upon the teacher and student are an insult to academic freedom. It imposes commonality on us all, rather than releasing each of us to pursue excellence. The goal of good education should be the pursuit of what is best. Not the protection or the propagation of what is common.

Common Core is a dumbing-down of education to what is common and average for all. Elites dictate what the teacher will teach. Good education has never been about diminishing inquiry to a group of ideas agreed upon by the powerful and the popular. The goal of the educator should be the pursuit of truth, not the embrace of what is common. Education should be about an open mind that challenges the consensus rather than a set of closed constructs of commonality that capitulate to the mediocrity of the group, and the collective opinion.

My faculty do not need to be told how to develop their syllabus or what textbooks to use to teach Economics 101. I don't tell them. No college faculty would ever accept being told by their college president what and how to teach so why would we ever want the government to tell good teachers what to teach? I trust my faculty to be good teachers and good scholars. Yet, when it comes to elementary and secondary education, we're supposed to think education should be dictated from the outside?

I'm against Common Core because I believe in intellectual integrity. The integration of head and heart and fact and faith that is directed by the student's thirst for truth and not the state's hunger for control. I am against Common Core because I believe in the liberal arts, I believe in liberty and liberation and freedom:

a free mind, a free man, rather than one held in bondage by politics and power and what is popular or what is common. I'm against Common Core because I believe in the humility of the student not the arrogance of the state. I'm against Common Core because I don't believe all paths are common or that they all lead to the same summit. I believe some paths lead to danger and death and some lead to safety and salvation. And as an educator I believe it's my obligation to help my students and my culture distinguish between the two.

I am against Common Core because I believe it's antithetical to the history of liberal education for educators to celebrate the mindless march of lemmings careening over a cliff of commonality. I believe the Pied Piper's tune of "Popular Opinion" can be one of common deception rather than one of personal discernment. I am against Common Core because I'm tired. I'm tired of the politically correct and boringly predictable *ad hominem* attacks used to call the questioning voices, such as mine, *stupid* and *ill-informed*.

I'm tired of the *ad populum* fallacies implicit in the word *common*. I am against Common Core because of the inevitable assumption of mediocrity that has already resulted in many of its proponents not understanding the basic Socratic logic I just used. I don't celebrate what's common. I just don't. I refuse to. I don't reward you for mediocrity. I don't slap you on the back when you graduate after four years of education and say, "Congratulations, you've measured up to the constructed consensus, to the common opinion."

I am against Common Core because, as an educator, I recognize that when we exchange the truth of God for a lie, we build a house of cards that will fall to mankind's insatiable lust for power and control.

The authority for education needs to go back to the local communities. Now that puts a lot of burden on parents, school boards, superintendents, and teachers—which is where it belongs. It belongs with the people who care about kids the most. We cannot abandon standards. But the question is, who's going to set them, who's going to define them, and who's going to decide what ideas are good or bad, right or wrong, true or false for your culture and for our kids? What is taught today in the classroom will be practiced tomorrow in churches, corporations, and the culture.

There's a reason for the mess we're in today—bad ideas. Bad ideas in society most often come from the top down, not from the bottom up. As a parent and lifelong learner, I believe our children's journey should be guided by the immutable, the permanent, and the true, not by the transient constructs of popularity, politics, and power. Our children will only succeed when we place our confidence in truth, and not in what is common.

12

SEX IN THE FAMILY

Sex used to be considered sacred. Now it is treated merely as a matter of common consumption on our college and university campuses. Intercourse, once guarded as an exclusive moral bond between a committed and faithful husband and wife, is now regarded as an amoral decision of little more consequence than whether or not one chooses prime rib or salmon for dinner, or whether to have eggs and bacon for breakfast. It is nothing more than casual recreation. Having sex with someone is now simply a matter of personal taste and preference with almost no concern for the other person. Far from sacramental, what was once thought of as "the marital act" is now treated as the necessary satiation of a human animal's appetite and is viewed as being about as special as a night of playing cards or going bowling.

This account from a college student captures the casual nature with which sex is treated in today's academy: "I woke up at three in the morning one day last year to my roommate having sex in his bed five feet away from me.... I realized what was going on...recognized the voice of the girl.... I had two classes with her the semester before and one that semester.... The next morning...there was no awkward exchange. No childish giggling. I simply told him that I could not believe that she didn't mind having sex with someone for the first time while someone else was in the room sleeping. I also couldn't believe that she hadn't stopped and covered herself up when I had walked out of the room. My roommate looked at me with a casual smile, the same smile I'd seen when talking about the Mets or Red Sox, the same smile I'd seen at our dining-room table over Taco Bell, and he said to me, 'Whatever, she's a college girl.'"[1]

No wonder we've stopped defending the very existence of the female. Whereas our culture once treated women as worthy of great dignity—as human beings of special status who should be honored and respected—we now treat them like fast food or a trip to the ballpark. How demeaning. How harmful to a young woman's emotional well-being. How damaging to her sense of self-worth. She is no longer a prize to be pursued and protected, but merely an object—just a "college girl"—to be used and discarded by one young man after another as he goes about his daily routine of satiating his desires.

Meaningful relationships have been supplanted by simple recreation. Co-eds are now just human products to be used for copulation. As Walker Percy said, "The so-called sexual revolution is not, as advertised, a liberation of sexual behavior but rather its reversal. In former days... sexual intercourse was the natural end and culmination of heterosexual relations. Now one begins with genital overtures instead of a handshake, then waits to see what will turn up (e.g., might become friends later). Like dogs greeting each other nose to tail and tail to nose."[2]

But that's not the worst of it. The story above is actually old news. It was told in 2005 by Vigen Guroian in an article in *Christianity Today* titled "Dorm Brothel: The new debauchery, and the colleges that let it happen." Since that time, our situation has not improved. The debauchery is now more openly sanctioned and even protected—although the insanity that ensues often leaves students dazed, damaged, and confused.

For example, Nathan and Melanie (not their real names) were students who "hooked up" on Memorial Day weekend in 2014 on the campus of my alma mater, Michigan State University (MSU).[3] The hookup began in the backseat of a car but was interrupted by a passerby. After they were interrupted, Melanie "revealed that the incident brought up unpleasant memories of a previous abusive relationship." So they both agreed not to continue. Later that night, Nathan tried again, reaching underneath Melanie's shirt to touch her breast. When she said no, he stopped. The relationship, such as it was, ended shortly after that.

Almost a year and a half after the brief incident, Melanie had decided she was a man and was awaiting surgery to look the part. Sixteen months after her hookup, Melanie decided to file a complaint with MSU officials about Nathan's unwanted advance—not the heavy session in the car that was interrupted, nor the several similar sessions, but the "one-time, non-consensual touching" that happened shortly afterward. The advance, both agree, stopped when she said *no*.

Why did Melanie choose to bring it up now? She feared an encounter with Nathan when using the male restrooms on campus. This is the mind-boggling madness we are left with when we declare biological truth no longer matters and sex is common as a handshake. Reality, however, does not bend to our degenerate whims.

As a result of the complaint, Nathan was punished by the school under Title IX federal rules that went into effect *after* the alleged incident. Although he has been accused of no crime by local authorities, the case has continued for two and a half years and shows no signs of ending soon. Nathan's lawyer Deborah Gordon says, "The so-called sexual harassment is not really sexual harassment. I have been doing these cases for more than thirty years. The breast touch occurred in the summer, off campus, the school was not in session, it had nothing to do with the school. Title IX does not require you to take cases when they don't involve the school." The incident will be on Nathan's permanent record, and he is required to divulge this information when he seeks employment.

Let me be clear: I am not defending his *or* her behavior. Yet both have been encouraged to engage in wanton sexuality by our hyper-sexualized campus cultures. Faculty and administration leaders alike cheer students on and ridicule all who dare suggest self-control or saving sex for marriage. Their hypocrisy knows no bounds. This story is but one of thousands that prove when traditional sexual standards are lost, when a biblical ethic is disparaged, it is always the woman who suffers first and most. Then it is not long thereafter that both men and women find themselves subjected to more laws (i.e. more rules than the church ever dreamed of) being imposed on them at the hands of duplicitous and arrogant elites who find it necessary to restrain the unwashed masses they seek to control.

When Donald Trump's crude comments about women surfaced during his presidential campaign, these progressive university folk were among the first to criticize him. The same people who tell their students anything goes when it comes to sex acted offended in order to score political points. I'm not defending his comments—not at all—but since when did they care about the adverse affects of objectifying women? Why should Trump's comments come as a surprise when many of those same professors champion "sex weeks" on their respective campuses, replete with seminars that include porn stars and even prostitutes as guest speakers? Doesn't the feigned shock expressed by the progressive Left seem just a bit disingenuous when we know as empirical fact this same faculty has no compunction at all about using similar vulgar language in their classes and would quickly belittle and shout down any "prudish" conservative such as me who tried to say otherwise?

Everything, from their celebration of *The Vagina Monologues* to the cover of *Cosmo* to the swimsuit edition of *Sports Illustrated* and nearly every beer commercial known to man, unapologetically portrays females as literal objects of sport to be enjoyed first and foremost for their body parts. So why the feigned outrage over Trump's comments?

While campuses protest the mere mention of Trump's name, they actively encourage students to discard traditional morality entirely. On the campus of the University of Oregon, a new app called SexPositive claims to help students eliminate shame and embrace sexuality as an experience that offers "the possibility for pleasure, intimacy, joy, and self-discovery, either with another person or by yourself."[4]

The app's design is itself a reflection of a basic tenet of the reigning sexual ideology: sex is a depersonalized, genitally-focused activity that aims to achieve maximum personal pleasure. Forget that retro idea about how sex is a loving, intimate encounter between a man and a woman who have committed their lives, and their entire selves, to each other. Oregon's sex app conveys the premise of this new sexual ideology perfectly: the user's focus is quite literally on what goes where, how much pleasure it produces, and what the risks might be. A sex app user first selects a body part or object from a menu, and then digitally spins a wheel to match his or her selection to another body part or object. (The list of objects intended for sexual use includes things like "anal plugs" and other "toys" as well as everyday objects that indulge odd sexual fetishes. Not for the squeamish.) Once the sexual "tools" are selected, the user navigates the touchscreen to select more information about how and where to use the chosen implements, to learn what "safer sex" precautions are recommended, and to assess the associated risks for sexually transmitted diseases. The app is adaptable to gay, straight, or undeclared folks, and suited for individuals, couples, or multiples—which suggests, of course, that the University of Oregon thinks it is perfectly natural for gender to be undeclared and for sex to be a multi-player game.

Bad ideas about sexuality, propagated for decades by faculty and university leaders, have produced a culture rife with bad physical consequences. Do we really want 25 percent of the millennial-age, female population to suffer from a sexually trans-mitted disease (STD)? How is this *pro-woman*? The Centers for Disease Control (CDC) 2015 data shows the number of cases for "gonorrhea, chlamydia and syphilis in the United States reached an unprecedented high in 2015—and people age 15 to 24 accounted for a large number of these new cases. There were over 1.5 million new cases of chlamydia, about 395,000 new cases of gonorrhea and nearly 24,000 cases of syphilis. The 15-24 age group accounted for 53 percent of gonorrhea cases and 65 percent of chlamydia cases. Syphilis was most commonly found among men who had sex with other men."[5]

The number of AIDS cases shows a similarly disturbing increase. According to the CDC, "Youth aged 13 to 24 accounted for more than 1 in 5 new HIV diagnoses in 2014. Young gay and bisexual males accounted for 8 in 10 HIV diagnoses among youth in 2014. At the end of 2012, 44% of youth ages 18 to 24 years living with HIV did not know they had HIV. In 2014, an estimated 1,716 youth aged 13 to 24 were diagnosed with AIDS, representing 8% of total AIDS diagnoses that year."[6] But we hear little about these dire consequences. The results are often swept under the rug to keep up the illusion that all is well.

The government's response to the growing rate of HIV, AIDS, and STDs is to expand sex-ed programs. They're throwing the gasoline of taxpayer dollars on the fire and claiming it is water. Students at universities are being "educated" on how to have sex like rabbits, but they're only causing higher rate of diseases and destroying the cornerstone of civilization—the family. Even middle and secondary schools are providing pornography to students so that they can better embrace amoral consumption-based sexuality.

At a middle school in suburban Denver, Colorado, students were "given access to extremely graphic sexual and homosexual pornographic material encouraging them to become sexually and homosexually active, descriptions of sex toys, and BDSM information." I personally interviewed one of the families involved to verify the story. What's even worse is some parents complained, but were "rebuked, intimidated, and even threatened by school officials—and ignored by elected school board members."[7]

We can stop AIDS and STDs right now. It's not complicated. Stop having unbiblical sex. These diseases are perpetuated through behavior. But we don't teach good behavior anymore, because we have kicked character, moral, and ethical development to the curb. Don't we believe in encouraging people to live healthy lives? Do we really believe it's fair that men who act on same-sex attraction be victimized by a disease disproportionately their own? Shouldn't we tell them they're making themselves ill? We have no problem telling smokers they're killing themselves. We tell the alcoholic to get help and stop drinking. We tell the obese to quit downing cookies and even levy taxes to discourage them from chugging super-sized colas, but mum's the word when it comes to ideas and consequences involving sex. Why?

BAD IDEAS = BAD FAMILIES

The reality is our buying in to false realities about sex has produced horrific cultural consequences. Because we don't want to talk about it, we create "safe spaces" where we can run from the problem instead of facing the pain of solving it. Many of the sex-related issues we're facing today started with the breakdown of the family. Shouldn't the government focus on solving the foundational family problem first? Shouldn't we start by addressing the issue of good parenting and male responsibility? Shouldn't men be taught to treat women as spouses and not recreational objects? Shouldn't we teach our sons to love and respect women instead of objectifying them?

What is all of this sexual promiscuity doing to the family structure? It's causing rising divorce rates, increases in unhealthy lifestyle choices, increases in childhood diseases, and other negative cultural effects.

Consider the impact of divorce, for example. Many people say children of divorced parents will outgrow the negative effects, but a study published by Penn State University, *Parental Divorce and Long-Term Harm to Children's Health*, found that "50-year-olds still feel the harmful effects of the parental divorces they experienced more than four decades earlier, effects evident in health impairments not shared by peers who grew up in intact families."[8]

Even Barack Obama, the product of a single-parent family, has said, "We know the statistics—that children who grow up without a father are five times more likely to live in poverty and commit crime; nine times more likely to drop out of schools and 20 times more likely to end up in prison. They are more likely to have behavioral problems, or run away from home or become teenage parents themselves. And the foundations of our community are weaker because of it."[9]

The erosion of objective moral standards has resulted in not only an increase in diseases and divorce, but also an increase in pregnancies outside of marriage. The result has been the deaths of countless millions of unborn children (with a disproportionate percentage being black and female) and a dramatic increase in single-parent homes. Yet we know that children reared in such dysfunction are statistically prone to live at a lower socioeconomic level. They also have a greater chance of being incarcerated, and are more prone to alcoholism and drug abuse.[10]

According the Pew Research Center, American Community Survey (ACS), and Decennial Census data, less than half of the kids in the United States live at home with mom and dad. Only 46 percent of children in the U.S. under the age of eighteen live in a home with two married heterosexual parents who are in their first marriage.[11] In 1960, that number was 73 percent. The trend is far, far worse among the African-American population.

Dr. Alveda King, niece of Martin Luther King Jr., is a staunch defender of the traditional family structure. Of the family, she says:

> I can assure you that the married-parent, natural family is a necessary component to achieve the American dream for African-Americans and for all of God's people. I know firsthand the importance of a strong family in overcoming difficulties; as a child I was jailed, my house was bombed, and my daddy and uncle were killed in the Civil Rights Movement of this great nation. If it had not been for the safety and security provided by my father and mother, we, their children, would have been severely if not irreparably traumatized.... Empirical research studies in the social science[s] point to family and marriage as the single most important factor in promoting economic justice, fighting poverty, and decreasing dependence on welfare.[12]

Many of our socioeconomic issues are directly linked to the health of the family structure. If the family structure falls in any civilization, the number of married couples decreases, economic mobility decreases, median family income decreases, child poverty increases, racial tension increases, and educational tensions increase.[13] The success and stability of an economy is directly related to the success and stability of the family structure. You cannot have one without the other. Eric Cochling of the Georgia Center for Opportunity puts it well: "To reinvigorate opportunity in America, we have to start by restoring the health and vitality of the American family. Nothing less will do."[14] If the family falls, so does the economy.

Many economic recovery programs and projects fail because they lack a focus on family restoration. The restoration of the married-parent family must be at the centerpiece of American life in order for a strong and successful economy, and society as a whole, to thrive. It is no coincidence that the English term *economy* originates from the Greek word *oikos*, which means *household*.

Social science data, as well as demographic and tax data, confirm intact families are more productive than any other type of living or household arrangement. Married-parent families work more. They earn more. They save more. They are more likely to qualify for a mortgage. They pay more in taxes. They are more likely to start and invest in a new business enterprise. They give more to charity. They volunteer more. They even vote more. They raise, on average, more children, the future lifeblood of any economy. And their children are more likely to attend and graduate from college, marry, and like their parents, raise productive children.

Federal welfare expenses have increased because the number of healthy families has decreased. According to the Heritage Foundation, welfare programs cost federal and state taxpayers $900 billion in 2010, enough to have awarded every three-person household living under the poverty level $50,000.[15] Over the next ten years, Heritage claims federal welfare spending will exceed $10 trillion. The bulk of this money gets spent to compensate for the disadvantages that stem from being raised in a broken home, living outside the protective bonds of marriage, or bearing children out of wedlock.

Even the future Social Security and Medicare deficits are related to a retreat from family life. Thanks to abortion (*Roe v. Wade*) and federal "family planning" (through Title X and Medicaid), we have fewer taxpayers to share the economic load. Even the Social Security actuary concedes this, claiming its projected deficits are caused "not because we are living longer, but because [average] birthrates dropped from three to two children per woman."[16]

Gary Becker, Nobel-prize winning economist, and economic expert on family, said "No discussion of human capital [and economic productivity] can omit the influence of families on the knowledge, skills, values, and habits of their children. Parents have a large influence on the education, marital stability, and many other dimensions of their children's lives."[17] In *The Wealth of Nations*, Adam Smith said, "The most decisive mark of the prosperity of any country is the increase in the number of its inhabitants," which he linked to "a numerous family of children."[18]

We don't need bigger government to solve these problems; we need a recovery of public policies that allow families to flourish again. If we really want to solve the many problems facing our nation today, let's stop growing the federal government and put our trust instead in the first and most basic unit of self-government—the family.

WHAT'S BEST FOR OUR CHILDREN?

The evidence is overwhelming that children in traditional families are much healthier and more prepared to make moral and just decisions than those who grow up with a single parent, grow up with a homosexual couple, and/or grow up in a situation of cohabitation (unmarried).[19] The media and educational systems should stop lying about the success of other "family" structures. The World Congress of Families has compiled a wealth of research and concluded:

> Married families are better off financially, socially, and health-wise than any other family structure. The intact married family has by far the most savings and wealth of all family structures (except for the widow with husband's insurance). Poverty rates are significantly lower among married families compared to cohabiting and single-parent families. Married families have the greatest net worth. Marriage has a significant positive impact on men's earning power. Men who are married increase their earning power, in general, by 27%.
>
> Children from intact married families outperform all the rest very significantly in school performance. Children from intact and always-unified families are less likely to be expelled from school than children of divorced parents or children from always-single mother families. Children from families that attend church weekly are more likely to finish high school and finish college or university. Children in married, two-parent families enjoy more economic well-being than children in any other family structure.[20]

The family structure with one mother and one father is the original design of the Creator of the universe. There is nothing that can replace a healthy family even though there are those who try to replace that structure with single-parent families or homosexual relationships.

The New Family Structures Study (NFSS) is the first to make a direct comparison of heterosexual with homosexual parents and use large, representative samples. Lead researcher Mark Regnerus published the first article based on the findings in the journal *Social Science Research* in June 2012. The Family Research Council summarizes the main findings of the study as follows:

- **Children do better when raised by their own, married mother and father.** Even *without* the data on children whose parents had same-sex relationships, the NFSS would be a significant contributor to the already large body of evidence showing the superiority of the "intact biological family" over all other household structures.

- **Children suffer when raised by homosexual parents**—not only in comparison to being reared by a married mother and father, but also in comparison to *all* other family structures. [That's not homophobic or hateful, just truthful. And speaking that truth shows compassion for children. Obscuring this truth is anything but loving.]

- **Homosexual relationships are intrinsically "unstable."** The fact that only two of over 200 children with a parent who had a same-sex relationship lived with that parent and his or her partner from birth to age 18 shows how extraordinarily rare "stable gay relationships" really are.

- **Public policy should continue to encourage the raising of children by a married mother and father,** while discouraging, attempting to reduce, and/or refusing to affirm or subsidize alternatives such as out-of-wedlock births, single parenthood, cohabitation, divorce, *or* homosexual parenting.[21]

Bad ideas about sexuality have resulted in bad results for the family. And many of those bad ideas originated on college campuses. They are certainly perpetuated and protected there today. As the historian Gertrude Himmelfarb observed more than a decade ago, "What was once stigmatized as deviant behavior is now tolerated and even sanctioned; what was once regarded as abnormal has been normalized. As deviancy is normalized, what was once normal is now considered deviant. The kind of family that has been regarded for centuries as natural and moral—the 'bourgeois' family as it is invidiously called—is now seen as pathological and exclusionary, concealing the worst forms of psychic and physical oppression."[22]

The family is the bedrock of a moral and just society. Without it, there would be no stability in the socioeconomic infrastructure of a culture. The data doesn't lie. A heterosexual married couple that raises a family will be the healthiest, most productive, and most stable for children. Instead of trying to destroy the family through wanton sex, colleges and universities should be trying to restore the sacredness of sex and protect the family rather than demonize it.

13

THANK GOD FOR THE CHURCH

In what must be one of the most ironic and intolerant moves by a leading university today, Princeton Theological Seminary, an allegedly Protestant school founded on Christianity, announced in March 2017 that it would be awarding Reverend Tim Keller the Kuyper Prize for Excellence in Reformed Theology and Public Witness—then they withdrew the award.

His crime? Expressing traditional Christian beliefs.

The president of the seminary, Rev. Craig Barnes, stated that by giving Keller the award it "might imply an endorsement of Keller's views against the ordination of women and LGBTQ people." But Keller's views are nothing new. They have been standard Church doctrine and policy for more than two millennia and are, likewise, still affirmed worldwide by most Christians to this day. It is Princeton that has shifted its definition of what it means to be Christian, not Keller.

Here we have an award named after Abraham Kuyper, a staunch defender of the same positions Keller holds, being withdrawn by Princeton's efforts to appease the tyranny of the gang. Before criticism began, the Kuyper Center for Public Theology praised Keller, saying he is "an innovative theologian and church leader, well-published author, and catalyst for urban mission in major cities around the world." Yet when pressured by the LGBTQ community and other ideological fascists of the progressive Left, they caved and compromised.

Nevertheless, Rev. Craig Barnes said—presumably with a straight face—he remains committed to academic freedom and "the critical inquiry and theological diversity of our community."[1] All Barnes and Princeton are doing is sacrificing truth, liberty, and justice for moral relativism, fantasy, and intellectual enslavement.

You don't have to agree with the specifics of my Christian faith to acknowledge that the Christian Church has been essential to much of what is good about Western civilization—and a positive influence on the rest of the world. Matthew Parris is a journalist for the *London Times*, award-winning author, and former Member of Parliament. He's also a gay atheist. "As an atheist," Parris said, "I truly believe Africa needs God."

Parris grew up in South Africa, and it was a return trip to Africa that prompted his comment. "In my return to my African heritage, I have realized that the continent of Africa, had it not been for Christian evangelism, would have suffered the fate of the machete, genocide, or the worship of Nike.... Missionaries, not aid money, are the solution to Africa's biggest problem—the crushing passivity of the people's mindset." Parris concluded it is Christianity's emphasis on a direct, personal relationship with

God that fuels an individuality that can "cast off a crushing tribal groupthink. That is why and how it liberates."[2]

A crushing, tribal groupthink—sounds a lot like the oppressive cultures we find on college campuses in America today. Here we have a gay atheist admitting Christian evangelism and its social and moral traditions have saved Africa from genocide, materialism, and scientism. Yet Princeton Theological Seminary discriminates against Christian leaders who embrace these social and moral traditions—and expects a better result. They are not alone. Many university leaders, faculty, and students insist on squelching any mention of God or the good the Church has done.

Even our Christian leaders seem intent on watering down the Christian faith to be more palatable to a generation that has lost its moral compass. Kendra Dean, a professor at Princeton Theological Seminary and author of *Almost Christian*, says contemporary culture has come to view Christianity as essentially nothing more than what she calls a "moralistic therapeutic deism."[3] God is being portrayed as an affirming "therapist" who is more focused on building up our self-esteem than confronting us with hard truths. Consequently, the reason many people are leaving the Church is they are receiving platitudes instead of preaching, acceptance instead of confrontation, and vague generalities instead of specific life direction. If all we want is a support group that will simply make us feel good about ourselves, we can find this in a myriad of places ranging from the yoga class at the local country club to Rotary, Kiwanis, or AA. Why turn to the Church?

THE GOOD IGNORED

Instead of trying to expunge any mention of the Christian Church from campuses, we should be extolling her virtues and proclaiming, "Thank God for the Church!" The truth is that few, if any, of the universities trying to kick out Christianity would exist without its influences. Chuck Colson said, "In every action we take we are either helping to create a hell on earth or helping to bring down a foretaste of heaven. We are either contributing to the broken condition of the world or participating with God in transforming the world to reflect his righteousness."[4] The Church has done more to bring a little heaven to earth than any other institution in history.

America's founders were fueled by a vibrant Christian faith. Even those who did not personally embrace it, acknowledged it as being essential for the formation and sustainability of the nation. In the 1830s, the American Church was part of forming the Underground Railroad to help runaway slaves escape to freedom. We remember the Underground Railroad, but our history books often neglect to mention the churches that stood against the cultural current for what they knew was right. Across the globe, it was Christianity that pushed to end slavery, a practice accepted as commonplace prior to Christians standing and demanding change. Likewise, in Germany the Pastor's Emergency League revolted against Hitler's control of the pulpits during World War II. Their courageous churches became known in history as "The Confessing Church" because of their stand against evil.

The Christian Church has been a force for humble boldness against evil in the world. It draws us by the power of the Gospel to a place of repentance in which we see how "the Way, the Truth and the Life" rescues us from ignorance and the blind tyranny of falsehoods. It calls us to carry the cross of Christ as we work to lighten the load of others. Above all, it is Christianity's clarion call to embrace the truth that empowers people to throw off the enslavement we all experience to our own fallen natures and to fight against the subjugation the powerful always seek to impose on the weak. Christianity warns us about the hazards of trusting ourselves too much. Christianity has been a true, noble, and good voice throughout history. Without Christianity, and its defense of truth, the world would be a much darker and controlled place—and the universities that now try to expel it from their campuses simply would not exist.

It is loving, merciful, and good for Christianity to thrive because it spreads truth. Our culture—every culture—needs the Church to rise up and be the Church. We are to love as Christ loved, serve as Christ served, and pursue righteousness, justice, truth, beauty, and goodness. It has not always been an easy decision for the Church to be all God called it to be. Yet for each time Christians have faithfully embraced their calling, history remembers them.

Today, the Christian Church needs to remember those previous generations. We must remind ourselves that the decisions to stand for truth, fight for justice, and teach goodness will not always be easy, but they will always be right. And although people will claim we are closed-minded because we claim there is only one way—we love them best when we communicate truth in love.

WHAT ABOUT PERFECT LOVE?

I have been asked within the Church how Christians should respond to the cultural shifts sweeping our land and the endless calls for tolerance and love. Because the university I lead is grounded in the Wesleyan tradition, several people have asked me if John Wesley's call to "perfect love" requires believers to be less "exclusive" in our community engagement. More directly, many have suggested Wesleyan charity implies political accommodation rather than confrontation and an openness to a "middle way," one of more tolerance and inclusion. As the leader of one of our nation's few remaining Wesleyan universities, here's my brief response to the Church and to all others who care to listen in.

First, it is true Wesley elevated love as evidence of God's grace in our lives. Loving God and loving our neighbor, however, demands that we hate sin, for sin always compromises our neighbor and sin always defies our God. John Wesley taught repeatedly that the obedient "methodical" path of Christianity is one that eschews disobedience at every turn. There is no place in Wesley's teaching to have a "conversation" about sin: Christian love demands we lead people to confess sin, not sit around and discuss it.

Second, Wesley was very clear about what he called "singularity," i.e. the exclusive non-negotiable claims of Christ and the Church. In fact, he made it so clear he said "singularity" was the difference between heaven and hell: "You must be singular or be damned. The way to hell has nothing singular in it. The way to heaven has singularity written all over it. You must be singular or be damned."[5]

Third, indeed, Wesley did say, "In the essentials unity...in all else charity," but in doing so he clearly made biblical "essentials" the top priority. In calling for "charity" he never intended to diminish the First Things. In fact, Wesley repeatedly preached that anyone who denied "the essentials" was guilty of being "almost Christian."

Fourth, Wesley's message elevated the dignity of what it means to be human. If he were with us today, he would be the first to say our inclinations do not and must not define us. He would condemn the dumbing down of a man and a woman to nothing but the sum of what they are inclined to do. He would shout that our identity is found in Christ, not in our proclivities and passions. Wesleyan/Methodist holiness means we rise above our appetites rather than capitulate to our every desire and instinct. John Wesley would cry out from today's pulpit, as he did from his own: *You are the imago Dei, not the imago dog! Now, by God's grace, act like it!*

Church leaders today should learn from John Wesley, who ran into the storm and not away from it. He did so with the confidence that if he won, great, that was God's grace, but if he lost, the battle was the Lord's and he was willing to go down fighting. He preached that compromise would be the Church's demise and if our salt "loses its savor" we will inevitably be "thrown out and trampled underfoot" by a culture laughing at our irrelevance. Bottom line: Wesley boldly confronted the leaders of his church and the leaders of his country and demanded they preserve culture, not take part in its rot.

Wesley would have this message for us today: "May God help us if we have really come to the point where we believe our salvation comes from negotiating a compromise with a world that hates our Lord and His Gospel." He would stand in the contemporary town square, as he did in his own, and shout: "There is no 'middle way' with Christ. He is the *only* way!" Have we reached that terrifying place in the story of the Church and as a country where we think our highest good is to negotiate a compromise with the world's way rather than to stand courageously with the Way of Christ?

I choose to stand with the many who still believe the answer is no! David and Barbara Green, founders of the craft store

Hobby Lobby, chose not to compromise when forced to fund abortions through the Patient Protection and Affordable Care Act. There are many who stand for biblical truth, but these choices, unfortunately, are becoming more frequent in our society. If you are a Christian institution, organization, or business, you are being singled out for silence.

The world will demand to know where you stand. You can momentarily avoid the backlash of name-calling, boycotts, fines, and possible closure, but, I would argue that in doing so, you have sold out rather than staked your ground. You have traded the truth for the temporary comfort of a lie and in the process destroyed the preserving cultural "salt" of the Gospel. The end result is as predictable as the sunrise: you will be thrown out and trampled underfoot for you have lost your savor and are of no meaningful value.

In a world rife with hatred, intolerance, human trafficking, and terrorism, even the secularists like Matthew Parris know this. The ultimate value of the Church is not found in therapeutic deism but in redemptive evangelism.

In the spring of 2016, Oklahoma Wesleyan University stood before the Supreme Court of the United States, forced to defend its female employees in a lawsuit against the Obama administration, the U.S. Department of Health and Human Services, and the regulatory abortifacient mandate being imposed upon us by the Affordable Care Act. More specifically, the pro-life women of Oklahoma Wesleyan joined with the Little Sisters of the Poor (a nationwide Catholic order of nuns dedicated solely to help the sick, the poor, and the dying) in saying they will not let the government intrude into one of the most private areas of their lives.

How can anyone argue that a free people should ever be subjected to federal prosecution and penalty for choosing not to participate in the supply and/or provision of reproductive products and services they don't want and would never use on moral grounds? How can anyone claim to be pro-woman and yet tell the women of the Little Sisters of the Poor and of Oklahoma Wesleyan University they are too stupid to decide what kind of contraception they do or don't want in their healthcare? How can anyone claim to be a feminist while at the same time capitulating to a federal government that declares it knows better than the individual female what drugs should be included in a woman's health insurance?

WHEN THE CHURCH FAILS TO LEAD

When I joined Bill O'Reilly on his show, he caught me by surprise when near the end of the interview he voiced his exasperation about the lack of Christian leadership in the face of the most defining cultural debates of our day. At the time, he was referring to uproar over the passage of the Religious Freedom Act in Indiana in 2015.

In the short time I had, my response was to give examples of rhetorical questions I think the Church should be asking, questions that expose the self-refuting, postmodern pablum of the progressive Left. For example, how is it tolerant to say, *I can't tolerate your intolerance*, and how isn't it hateful to say, *I hate you hateful people*?

I suggested the opponents of the Church seem more interested in ideological fascism than intellectual freedom. Opposition to Indiana's Religious Freedom Restoration Act (RFRA), for example, looked more like tyranny and forced agreement than the free, open, liberal, and tolerant exchange of ideas. I argued that we, as Christians, should boldly declare, "The emperor has no clothes" and, that in doing so, we would likely find our neighbor standing beside us (silently watching this sad parade) and agreeing. I concluded by arguing that truth always exposes deception and that by reclaiming and defending it, the Church always wins.

Mr. O'Reilly responded, "But Doctor, the big clerics are MIA. You must have the leadership that is going to take that philosophy you just described to the opposition and the leaders [of the Church] have not stood up." Since that interview, several people have asked what I would have said if I'd had more time to respond.

Well, here it is: *Mr. O'Reilly, you are absolutely right*!

Where is the Church leader willing to say that whether someone is Mormon, Muslim, Methodist, Buddhist, or Baptist she should not be forced to agree with or celebrate someone else's behavior that is contrary to her religious and moral convictions?

Where is the Church leader willing to stand up for freedom of religious liberty and ask the obvious: are these cultural issues of sexuality about identity or inclinations?

Where is the leader willing to say love is a much higher ethic than careless tolerance, and saying "I will tolerate you" is more of an insult than a compliment?

Where is the leadership willing to confront the prevailing politically correct narrative as nothing short of pedantic posturing that dumbs down the debate and conflates tolerance with tyranny, liberty with licentiousness, freedom with a free-for-all, and human dignity with human desire?

Where is the Chesterton of today to point out there is no liberty without law and no freedom without fences? Where is the Wilberforce to say we are men and not animals? Where is the Lewis to remind us we can do no measuring without a measuring rod *outside* of those things being measured? Where is the Wesley willing to confront the silly obfuscation of our time by saying, "This is mere playing with words. Explain your terms and the objection vanishes away"?[6]

Given a few more seconds on *The Factor* (or any other venue for that matter) I would have said, *Mr. O'Reilly you are absolutely spot on*! Indeed, the voice of the Church by and large is MIA. If it weren't, then leaders like then Governor Mike Pence of Indiana wouldn't feel as if they were standing alone with a finger in the dike, trying to hold back an impending disaster while the rest of the world walks by without caring that the cultural dam is about to burst.

As Christians, we can point fingers at the Church and its leaders, but there comes a moment when we must realize *we* are the Church. Even though we may not be pastors, priests, or preachers, each of us is a member of the Church and must be leaders of the Church. Each one of us forms critical members of the "body." Each of us is necessary to the function of the whole. The eye cannot say to the hand, I have no need of you. The head cannot say to the feet, I don't need you. When we fail to stand unified and confident for the self-evident truths endowed to us by our Creator—for the goodness of the Gospel—we amputate the body and show ourselves to be hypocrites of our own faith. We'll soon watch our culture and nation turn its back on us and slip away.

It's already happening.

The American Culture and Faith Institute (ACFI) recently conducted a study that asked Americans if they had a biblical worldview. There were six thousand people interviewed from three different populations and the surveys revealed troubling results.[7] George Barna, who directed the study for ACFI, said, "It's very important to know how many people have a biblical worldview because peoples' behavior is driven by their beliefs— we do what we believe."

The survey for the general public showed 10 percent of American adults *actually* have a biblical worldview as opposed to the 46 percent who *claim* to have one. That's a group of 88 million people who think they have a biblical worldview but, according to their answers in the survey, they do not. Barna said the questions "collected information about attitudes and behaviors related to practical matters like lying, cheating, stealing, pornography, the nature of God, and the consequences of unresolved sin."

The second survey was for theologically conservative, Protestant pastors. It used the same questions as the general public survey. The outcome for this survey was that 88 percent of the test group qualified as having a biblical worldview.

The third survey used the same measurement indicators to gauge the "SAGE Cons," Spiritually Active, Governance-Engaged Conservative Christians. The results showed that 90 percent of the SAGE Cons were committed Christian disciples, even higher than the conservative Protestant pastors.

The three surveys revealed a wealth of fascinating data about our culture and the Christian faith:

- Not surprisingly, given the state of colleges and universities today, the younger an adult is, the less likely he is to have a biblical worldview. Among adults eighteen to twenty-nine years old, just 4 percent were committed Christians. The number rose to 7 percent among those in the 30–49 age bracket; doubled to 15 percent among the 50–64-year-olds; and peaked at 17 percent among those sixty-five or older.

- Three out of ten adults (30 percent) claim to be born-again Christians based on their decision to confess their sins and accept Jesus Christ as their savior. However, among that segment of Americans less than one-third (31 percent) emerged as being committed Christians.

- Overall, one-third of adults (32 percent) described themselves as theologically conservative. Among that group of 32 percent, just 25 percent qualified as committed Christians.

- While about half of the nation considers itself to be "pro-life advocates," the survey discovered that just 19 percent of them are committed Christians.

- The survey found that while about one out of every ten adults (11 percent) claims to read the Bible daily, less than half of them (45 percent) fit the framework of a committed Christian.

The ACFI data highlights the fact that although pastors seem to understand what it means to live biblical lives, the rest of the nation doesn't even understand basic Christian doctrines. This disconnect leads to misperceptions about the role of the Church in culture. This gap is especially true for young people whose only exposure to Christianity in schools is often negative. Is there any more pertinent poster child of this problem than a student who actually complains about a biblically-based sermon about love because it made him feel uncomfortable?

We've come to think that the responsibility of the Church is to make people comfortable, but that was never its purpose. The Church is supposed to proclaim truth. Truth does not worry about making people comfortable, or worry about not offending. The truth is often offensive because it reveals reality: the reality of the world and the reality of people. It shines a light on the bad and the evil in the world. Truth makes people uncomfortable because it exposes what they're doing in the shadows. This uncomfortable feeling is called guilt—and recognizing it is necessary for any sustainable society.

"Dear Christians, it's not the church's job to make us feel comfortable"[8] is how Matt Walsh titled an article responding to a pastor. The preacher said what many Christians say today:

> I'm a pastor and I have to say I've read your work for a while and I find it very troubling. There is no tolerance, inclusiveness, or love in your writings. It's hateful towards the LGBTQ community and others who don't share your views about gay rights, reproductive rights or many other issues. Matt, churches should be focusing on how to welcome people in, whether they happen to be gay, trans, feminist or any other group you denigrate. "Christians" like you and all the rest on the far right have pushed these people away for so long. Matt no matter what you or your ilk say in your backwardness and bigotry, Christians in a committed same-sex relationship and others in the LGBTQ community are following God's design for their lives. That's the message the church needs to spread. God is love. Love is love! Your message of hatred and exclusion should be left in the dark ages where it belongs. You should be ashamed. I will pray for you.

Walsh responded brilliantly:

> These aren't 'my views' about gay rights and 'reproductive rights,' as you refer to them. I am merely agreeing

with the One who has already made His position on these subjects known.... It's not the church's job to make us comfortable, pastor. Its job is to help to make us holy.

I agree with Walsh. The Church should love people enough to never enable their sin. When Jesus was crucified, one of the thieves renounced his sins and was granted access into heaven. The other thief was not similarly welcomed by Jesus, presumably because he did not renounce his sins. Should we now lecture Christ about not being inclusive enough?

Walsh reinforces the central message of Christianity—that all have sinned and fallen short of the glory of God: "Let's not focus this whole conversation on homosexuality and abortion and those kinds of issues. You bring them up, you focus on them, because you think special exceptions and dispensations should be made for the people in those groups. But I say *no one* gets a special exception from the repentance requirement—not liberals, not conservatives, not homosexuals, not heterosexuals, not you, and certainly not me."

We should be telling people what sin is and teaching them how to confess and repent from their sins. True love confronts. It does not allow people to continue to believe lies. I would say it's hateful to allow someone to continue living a lie. Truth gives hope. Truth sets us free. And the Church exists to help me face the truth about my weakness and help me become holy by God's grace.

APOLOGIES OR *APOLOGIA*?

Instead of confronting sin, the Church of today mostly seeks to apologize. Instead of giving a defense of the faith, an apologia as Scripture calls it, we give apologies. The same goes for Christian schools and universities who are self-deprecating to their own embarrassment and even demise. They seem to strive for mediocrity as if average is a sign of humility. They never say they're the best. They never express themselves with confidence. All the marketing material and messaging screams, "We're second best!" It should not be so.

I'm not saying Christians should be arrogant or boastful, but it's neither when we present ourselves and our Savior as being better than the alternative. The apologizing happens because of a twisted sense of guilt. But we have been forgiven, and now serve as ambassadors of Christ on a mission of reconciliation. It is endemic in the Christian character to be humble, but too many Christians today take humility to the negative extreme.

Consequently, we keep apologizing. We're sorry for the Crusades. We're sorry for the Inquisition. We're sorry for the hypocrisy. We're sorry for slavery. We're sorry for all of it. Yes, there were Christians who did things that were wrong during the Inquisition and during the era of antebellum slavery, but the Church is also the force that corrected those evils. Why then are we not confident and courageous about the long history of good the Church has done? Why then do our pastors not take greater confidence in the veracity of Scripture and in the track record of the Church?

The Gospel of Christ is not a quest for mediocrity, yet that's the mission the Church seems to embrace today. Why dwell on a few wrongdoings by some, when the Church has done such fabulous work? We've rescued women from sexual slavery. We've established and organized hospitals. We've established the educational system. We've established orphanages. Does the average pastor even know that, or is he too busy apologizing for Christianity?

Many Christian leaders don't realize the ideas of Christianity are the foundation of economic freedom and free enterprise. If you don't have religious freedom, you soon will not have economic freedom.

Instead of apologizing all the time, we should be providing an *apologia*, a defense of our positions, the truth about the good the Christian Church has done. We should be confident and pursue excellence because we have direct access to the Source of all truth. We can be excellent and step forward with courage, because we know what's right. Think about it: when the best college football teams in the nation take the field, do you see either of them apologizing for offending the other team by believing they are the better team? Of course not. Then why should the Church apologize for knowing and proclaiming truth?

I'm passionate about this because it is the heart and soul of what we've done at Oklahoma Wesleyan. We've pushed back against this feigned humility epidemic in a lot of the Evangelical movement. They don't even make the case for Christianity. They just apologize. The Church should be bold in trying to help people by delivering the truth to a troubled culture. It should be bold, but it often is not. It's not just the universities that have become day cares. In spite of Jesus' claim that the gates of hell would not prevail against it, much of the Christian Church today has also chosen coddled over courageous and become crowd-pleasers rather than Christ-followers.

14

ADVICE FOR CONCERNED PARENTS

"Amy wants to go home," one of my Resident Assistants (RAs) told me. It was orientation time and I was head of student affairs at another university some years ago. We told concerned parents we were going to keep their kids busy so they wouldn't get homesick. From dawn until dusk we had games and activities to help them get plugged in before classes started. But by day two, Amy (not her real name) wanted to go home.

"Tell her to hang on for a couple of days," I told the RA, "and she'll be fine. The homesickness will pass soon." After the RA left to pass along my message, I checked Amy's record and discovered she was from Arizona (and the college I was working for at the time was in the Midwest). She simply can't go home, I thought, she has no way to get there from here.

But when the RA returned the next day, nothing had changed. Amy still wanted to go home.

After Amy came to the office, I discovered she was a delightful young lady. She seemed extroverted and engaged and in many ways a perfect fit for our campus community. I repeated all the things the RA said to her about encouraging her to give it more time, but to no avail. So I decided to be more serious about her situation.

"Look, Amy, you're from Arizona. There's no way you can buy a plane ticket today and go home. It'll cost over $1,000 one way. You're going to have to stay for a week or so to acclimate to the new environment. I guarantee by the time that's over, you'll be fine." I thought I was helping her deal with the reality of her situation in a way that would help her confront and overcome her fears or discomfort.

"Oh, that's no problem," she said, reaching into her purse. She pulled out a one-way plane ticket, given to her by her mother, just in case she couldn't make it through the first few days of college orientation. Amy stepped onto that plane, and I never saw her again. How could she have given up so easily? Simple. Her mother gave her *a ticket to fail.*

I tell this story every year during our new parent orientation. The moral of the story is this: *parents, don't give your kids a ticket to fail.* Instead, here are four things parents should do if they want to educate their children effectively and prepare to help them succeed in the real world instead of producing more snowflakes.

1. STOP PUTTING THEM ON THE WRONG TRAIN

Parents, let me be blunt. Stop sending your kids off to institutions that teach the narcissistic postmodern pablum of moral nihilism, self-actualization, and multi-cultural syncretism and, thus, encourage your sons and daughters to live in fantasyland instead of reality. You are responsible for where you send your kids to school. If you keep sending them off to institutions that idolize the created rather than the Creator, and that take great pride in politically correct nonsense, you're going to get the predictable results of these terrible ideas and terrible behaviors.

Search for universities that haven't sold their souls. Search out schools (very few though they may be) that honor and celebrate the self-evident truths endowed to us by our Creator. Find the college that defends the time-tested propositions of God rather than the dozens of institutions that seem so eager to perpetuate the transient constructs of man. Look for the university that is classically "liberal" and that seeks to "conserve" the things that matter most in mankind's march for liberty and liberation.

Search high and low for the school that believes in conserving the life of an unborn child more than that of an owl, a tree, or a whale. Find the college that stands boldly for the objective definition of what it means to be a man or a woman—for the empirical reality of what it means to be a female. Find the university willing to go down fighting for truth in the battle to conserve the First Things—the most important things—the ideas that matter. Settle for nothing less than an academic institution committed to teaching your children the objective, revealed, and proven fact—of the *imago Dei*.

Please, parents, take this seriously. When you choose higher education for your eighteen-year-old son or daughter, remember all I've said in this book: ideas matter. Ideas do have consequences.

The orientation process is a great indicator for determining the priorities of a college. Orientation is usually a three-day process where the student rolls up, mom and dad unpack the bags, and everybody celebrates. The student is then given a schedule for all the fun and games they're going to do for the first couple of days. These first few days are intentionally designed to keep the student busy, so he or she won't get homesick, and there are usually some courses and group meetings so students can learn more about life on campus, how to navigate the university's various resources, and how to live with other students.

However, one thing I've often told parents is this: when you drop your kids off at most schools, what you've spent eighteen years of your life "training up your son or daughter in the way they should go so when they are old they will not depart," your school of choice is gleefully and intentionally tearing down in the first eighteen minutes of their time on that campus. As you unpack their bags, leave them at the ivory tower, turn, and drive away, it will only be a few minutes before someone is telling your children that your ideas are silly and undesirable.

Why in the world would any good parent do that? Why in the world would you leave your child at a school that takes great pride in tearing the heart, mind, and soul out of your kid in the first few seconds as you're driving away? It makes no sense. If you're paying for your child's schooling, you're simply throwing away tens of thousands of dollars to have some arrogant professor or dean undo all you did. If you've spent all this time training your child and then think it's okay to drop him off at such schools and all will be well, you are wrong. It won't be.

Most freshman courses at secular and even Christian schools focus on forcing a nihilistic worldview on your kids as soon as the school can. That's where this train starts to go off the rails. The majority of faculty are very progressive today. In fact, 60 percent of professors identify as very liberal, 28 percent identify as moderate, and only 12 percent identify as conservative.[1] These people are teaching your children. We wonder why our country is crippled? It's because our schools have been taken over by professors who believe in micro-agressions, trigger warnings, safe spaces, moral nihilism, and all other things politically correct.

The majority of colleges and universities strip away traditional values and the very concept of moral truth as soon as the freshman gets on campus. At most universities, freshmen orientation is no longer simply a time to become acquainted with friends, learn about college life, and receive instruction on how to succeed in class. Instead, it should be called re-orientation. At Columbia University, for example, orientation has been redesigned to give students the chance to "reevaluate and...rid themselves of their own social and personal beliefs that foster inequality."[2]

In other words, your sons and daughters are told, in the first few minutes of their college experience, before the boxes are unpacked or they even know where their first class will be held, to "rid themselves" of anything that smacks of a conservative or Christian worldview. They are encouraged to set aside their "personal belief" in natural law, common sense, and traditional morality—anything grounded in the exclusive claims of orthodox Christian faith—because that belief might smack of "inequality." They are told they must be "tolerant" of all worldviews except those the faculty and administration now watching over them deem intolerable—a double standard that is surprisingly void of recognition.

Lest there be any confusion as to the intent of such re-orientation programs, noted philosopher and professor Richard Rorty, who served at such noted institutions as Wellesley College,

Princeton University, University of Virginia, and Stanford University, sums it up best: "[Parents] we are going to go right on trying to discredit you in the eyes of your children, trying to strip your fundamentalist religious community of dignity, trying to make your views seem silly rather than desirable."[3]

The goal of most universities today is not to orient students but, rather, to re-orient them; not to educate students but rather to re-educate them. It's a goal that sounds eerily like something you would expect to read in a novel by Orwell or Huxley, but not exactly what you thought you were getting when you read that pretty, four-color college brochure that promised you the best American education has to offer. Maybe it's time to find out what's really going on before you put your kids on the wrong train—and you both pay a high price for it.

2. START ASKING THE RIGHT QUESTIONS

I'm often asked by parent or grandparents, "How do I decide if a certain college is right for my child?" My advice is to meet with the president of the school. If he won't meet with you, that tells you a lot. You're paying a lot of money. If the president won't meet with you, do you really want to go there? But, if he or she will meet with you, ask at least two critical questions.

Question number one: *What is your view of the Bible*? Question number two: *What is your view of truth*? Then be quiet and listen. Does he say Scripture is inerrant, infallible, and authoritative? If he does, good answer. He believes in the authority of God's word. Does she say truth is an objective reality revealed by God and not a post-modern construct of man? If she says that, good answer. Now, if they don't say either one of those things, keep asking until you get the clarity you need. If they dodge your questions entirely, it's not because they are stupid and don't know why you asked. It's because they don't want to answer you. If they act as if they don't understand your questions, please don't believe them. They do. They're just hoping you won't ask any more questions before agreeing to pay them.

The president is the reflection of the school. Jesus tells us, "You shall know them by their fruits" (Matthew 7:16). What kind of fruits is the university producing? Is it teaching the authority of revelation and the reality of truth? As a Christian, I find these two questions to be the most important for understanding an educator's character and viewpoints. What educators believe informs how they lead and influence other people. It provides an indication of how they're equipping students—your students—to go out into the world. Don't stop asking questions until you know that you know where the university stands on ideas that matter.

3. INVEST WISELY IN THEIR PREPARATION

A lot of parents look at different colleges for the wrong reasons. They only care about making sure their child gets a good-paying job or figuring out which college is cheaper than another. Their focus is often on pragmatic utility rather than the principles of truth and morality. Too many parents think, *My kid needs to go to this particular secular college that doesn't align with our values at all in order to get the career he wants. He'll be fine. He just must suck it up for four years, keep his head down, get the credentials, and get out.* There are times when that approach is warranted—if survival is your aim. But a student trying to survive will find it difficult to truly thrive.

Too many parents settle for survival. A mother who was wrestling with these decisions once told me, *We think we can send him off to [a well-known secular school] because there are campus ministries there and he can get involved in a good church, so he'll be ok. What do you think?*

My response was essentially this: let's assume you're right. Let's assume you send him off to this prestigious school and he gets involved in a para-church organization. Let's assume he stays involved in a good, Bible-believing church, and, as a result, he doesn't get involved in the party scene, get addicted to drugs, get drunk all the time, get anybody pregnant, or contract an STD. Let's assume all of that. Four years later he graduates having stayed out of trouble. Is that your measure of success and what you wanted out of his college experience?

If so, aren't you setting the bar awfully low? Just because he avoided these dysfunctions and diseases, that doesn't mean he received a good education. Isn't education supposed to teach more than that? Shouldn't a good education expose him to the total truth? And are you really going to measure the success of his education based on his avoidance of immorality and sexually transmitted diseases? If so, I'm not too sure what value you're placing on education.

If he goes there, are they going to teach him any more about God and the revelation of His truth? No. He'll get an education in accounting, for example, but he'll know nothing about why and how God and His eternal truths apply to accounting. Since when did education become only about avoiding the bad?

Another common complaint I get from concerned parents is they can't afford to send their children to private Christian or similar schools. Often the enticement of "free money" from state institutions is just too much to ignore or resist. But I often wonder what they're spending recreational cash on and is it more important than their child learning more about the immutable time-tested truths of God, rather than learning less? There are some parents who won't hesitate spending money on a new car, on a boat, on a second home. Are these things more important than their child's education?

On the other end of the spectrum are parents who truly do not have much money. When they compare tax-supported state university tuition to a private school, they think they have only one option. But the reality is this: that private college is probably going to discount tuition in some way by approximately 50 percent on average. If that is still too much, most students will qualify for Pell Grants, scholarships, and similar aid. And most students can secure low-interest loans that will pay for themselves over time. So at the end of the day, you're probably going to pay only a few thousand dollars more than at the state college. Is your child's future worth a few thousand dollars to you? Is it worth a couple grand to keep them from learning a bunch of politically correct nonsense and moral obfuscation at another school? It is to me, but then I'm committed to doing all I can to ensure my sons are well prepared, not just to survive, but to thrive.

The data shows 70 percent of the students you send off to the state university will lose their faith by the time they're juniors.[4] Some of those students come back to the faith, but it's not a lot. Many students leave because they don't know what to believe, their views changed, they dislike organized religion, or they're unsure what to believe,[5] no thanks to the fact that they've spent the past four years in a community that disparages the assumption of truth, mocks the concept of morality, and laughs at even the thought of character development. Are you going to bet the farm your kid is in the 30 percent who stay committed?

Unfortunately, most parents do. Even many homeschooling parents who sacrifice everything for those first eighteen years often become over-confident and think getting their child into a secular school somehow affirms their homeschooling prowess. They send their students to secular schools and watch it all get washed away by political indoctrination.

The educational path we choose says something about what we believe. T. S. Eliot once said, "In choosing one definition [of education] rather than another we are attracted to the one because it fits better with our answer to the question: What is man for?"[6] Our educational paradigms flow directly from the biases we hold concerning the very definitions of who we are, why we are here, and what we are obligated to do about it.

If, for example, you believe we are mere fleshy *bags of biology* and nothing but the products of happenstance and chance, then your view of education will likely take on a certain utilitarian hue. However, if you have a view that believes all human *beings* are created equal and in the image of God and as the result, regardless of race, sex, or age, we all have certain unalienable rights, you will seek an educational "fit" that will inculcate certain responsibilities and duties accordingly to the generations that follow.

Parents, be warned: there is no such thing as "value neutral" education—yes, even at Yale and Oklahoma Wesleyan University. No professor enters the classroom without an agenda. But the question must be asked, is education about obtaining a career or acquiring character? Is a degree about earning more money or instilling more morality?

The best education is a classical liberal arts education, and it is one that results in liberty and liberation in a free people and free society. It differs from indoctrination only to the degree it is free of intimidation, honors open inquiry, and guards tenaciously the right to defy the capriciousness of a king or the consensus of the crowd. True education fears the truth but never the tyrant.

4. TRAIN THEM TO KNOW THE TRUTH

I've heard some parents justify sending their students to secular schools by saying, *My child is a missionary.* Why throw them into the fire without first teaching them how to fight fire with water, or lies with truth? But training them to know the truth should neither start nor end at the college campus. I recommend parents invest in worldview and apologetics training camps with their teens so they can learn how to defend their worldview and how to argue for truth effectively. It's as simple as doing an online search for "Christian worldview training." A lot of them are rigorous, thorough, and intellectually challenging. I can assure you they're not learning this information from most churches. Most church youth groups are having pizza parties rather than discussions about how to defend their faith.

A lot of what we see happening on college campuses is a result of poor child rearing. The education of a child starts way before college. We have a coddled generation because parents have rejected the original doctrine of sin as we discussed earlier. We believe a utopian society can be achieved. One where no one is ever "offended" and children are not born sinful, but rather in need of being made to feel "comfortable." We have done this to such an extent that public policy is following in line with public culture.

When you acknowledge that sin is real and the world is full of evil, you realize it is impossible to enact "safe spaces" around our children and achieve a world where no one is ever offended and every individual person's "trigger warnings" are considered. The world does not function this way. It is broken. Evil exists. Sin is real. And by and large America has sheltered its children from this harsh reality.

Chuck Colson said, "Nowhere does the clash of worldviews have greater social impact than in the denial of sin and the consequent loss of moral responsibility. As Christians we need to learn to detect false ideas and to show why they are wrong. For if we fail to recognize prevailing worldviews, the worst that may happen is that we ourselves will be sucked into false thinking unawares—and lose our distinctive message."[7]

We have squelched the feelings of guilt in our children and as a consequence greatly mitigated their ability to feel like they have done something terribly wrong. We have taught millennials, "It's not your fault" and they actually appear to believe it! If we do not allow our next generation to experience the reality of sin in their lives and experience the corresponding guilt, however unpleasant it may be, then we will have created a culture with no understanding of virtue or vice and no concept of what it even means to be good or evil—one with no awareness of its own culpability and its own sin. In such a world everything is relative—good and bad, right and wrong are subject to personal interpretation with no measuring rod of truth.

We have eased their guilt by telling them it is always someone else's fault. The government. The coach. The teacher. The principle. Everything and everyone is to blame, but not our kids. When someone says something offensive, we rush in to rescue them and tell them they "shouldn't have to listen to that or go through that." We are trying to keep them from experiencing the hard realities of life. It won't work. Parents need to teach children that life sometimes includes hearing things we don't want to hear and doing things we don't want to do; things that make us feel uncomfortable and, yes, even things that make us feel unsafe at times.

We have not only coddled young people on their college campuses and in their childhood years at home, but we have also begun to allow this philosophy to permeate our culture. If you are a millennial who intuitively recognizes that something is terribly wrong with the trajectory of your generation and you want to withstand the current trend of "safe spaces" and trigger warnings—if you want to resist becoming a member of the coddled and comfortable club, remember this: we sometimes tend to think we know all we need to know. Yet often, our humble hearts can help us more than our proud minds.

Remember that we never really know enough until we recognize God alone knows it all. I implore you to not be too easily satisfied. Stop thinking you know everything. Don't be content with the safety of what you think you know. Don't accept being coddled intellectually but rather seek to be challenged. Run toward the dissonance of life. Wrestle with the ideas you find most discomforting. Look for the conflicts that will strengthen your resolve and mold your character. Do not seek to live in a world of continual ideological comfort; a world that assuages your guilt; or a world that ignores your sin. Instead, recognize that God is a confronter as much as He is a comforter and that He demands something incredibly risky and even dangerous. He demands that you become like Him! The answer is not found in the "safe spaces." The answer is found in the goodness of Christ.

To the parents—I encourage you to teach your sons and daughters the virtue of confession rather than the vice of complaining. Model healthy confrontation. Stop the coddling. Stop the enablement. Instill in your kids an ethic to work hard and expect nothing. Teach them to have difficult conversations, and do not shelter them from contrary ideas or a robust disagreement. Instead show them how to recognize lies and how to fight them with the power and principles of truth.

Instill in them a desire to see what is right exalted and what is wrong extinguished. Teach them to value free speech even when it is in opposition to their own opinions. Train them to have eyes to see the human dignity in every person, and *their* right to a contrary view, but also teach them to debate and defend their beliefs eloquently and articulately. Train them to think of others as higher and better than themselves—to show Christ's love for everyone—while also confronting them with the fact that no one is higher or better than Christ and that He alone is the definition of love. Challenge your son. Confront your daughter. Tell them this immutable fact: Jesus is the final measuring rod outside of those things being measured. If you want to be right, then submit to His rule. He alone knows the answers. He is not safe, but He is good.

15

THE UNIVERSITY LEADERSHIP VACUUM

Our university leaders and faculty need to grow a spine. Our times demand it. We have too many learned cowards lining once-hallowed halls of learning. Fewer and fewer voices have the courage to stand and speak the truth and simply say "I disagree." Those who dare to do so are ignored or silenced by the "tolerant" who deem the rare voice of dissent as intolerable. A professor at Wake Forest University admitted, "The problem is that whenever you are on the liberal left, to some degree, you don't really see conservative ideas as even valid or worth the time and effort to allow because you have a sense that you know more and you know better. This arrogance creates an 'ideological vacuum.' In this vacuum, professors do not acknowledge counter-arguments on issues or challenge their own assumptions."[1] Vapid leadership allows this ignorance to be the norm. A vacuum will be filled by something. In today's culture, it's being filled by snow-flake insanity, and our culture is paying a high price.

College and university presidents, board members, and faculty have let this travesty occur. Our schools are permeated with anti-Christian and nonsensical, dare I say *suicidal*, ideas. Even worse, Judeo-Christian words have been stolen. Love, freedom, equality, justice, truth, and compassion are all changing before our very eyes.

Too many academic leaders stand idly by, content to drink the Kool-Aid of false compassion. We have bought the lie that confrontation and compassion are antithetical rather than complementary. It's nonsense. In the Christian faith, God tells us He disciplines those He loves and discipline is rarely pleasant. He doesn't say He refrains from disciplining *because* He loves. Discipline and love are complementary, not antithetical. Our unwillingness to help students by confronting and disciplining them reveals our lack of love for them. We don't coddle because we care about students. We coddle because we don't care enough to bother. We care more about our own feelings of comfort or desire to be popular than their growth and readiness for the challenges of real life. Confrontation is not synonymous with hate. Any decent parents know if we love our kids, we'll confront them. Failing to confront will result in them compromising body, mind, and soul.

But today we have parents who don't know how to rear or confront their children properly. We have professors who don't know how to confront their students with good ideas and challenge their bad ideas. We have college presidents who get caught like deer in the headlights when there's a cultural conflict. They don't want to call a spade a spade because they're afraid of being labeled *haters*. Search online for university presidents who will take a stand for truth, and you'll find a very short list of those willing to stand tall in the face of the snowflake rebellion.

Sadly, even evangelical Christians, who are supposed to be the ones proclaiming the truth, either stand by and do nothing or actively attack those with the courage to stand. The fact is the overwhelming majority of negative comments about my "This is not a Day Care" post came from those in the Church and not from the secular world. Our statistical analysis showed that, of all the comments from the 3.1 million views of the story in the first couple weeks, 97 percent were positive. The atheists and the secularists wrote to say, *Thank you. This needed to be said.* It was the church administrator, the pastor, and the Christian college professor who fancied himself as smarter than thou, who said, *This message was too harsh and confrontational.*

Their criticism simply proved my point. Their solution was to criticize me for being too critical; to confront me for being too confrontational; to write a blog about tolerance while calling my blog intolerable; to call upon the Church to coddle sin rather than to confess it. They seemed to think the best rebuttal to my public critique was to write their own public critique rebutting public critiques. They seemed only too ready to argue that comfort is more important than repentance and support is more important than challenge. Their solution was and is to coddle and enable more—to confront and challenge less.

I hardly even need to respond. Any schoolboy can see the self-refuting nature of their argument. Even a self-described atheist from the psychology department at the University of Central Florida wrote, "I don't agree with your religion, but thank you for saying what needs to be said...Please carry on!" While much of the secular world recognizes the lunacy of *safe spaces*, the Church condemns those who love young people enough to speak the truth and confront them. Sad. Shameful. And I would argue, even sinful.

Christ told us when the salt loses its savor it is rightfully considered useless and thrown out. Could it be His Church has lost its salinity to the point that secular folks now simply disregard our message as tasteless mush? Could it be that the edacious response to my post—and perhaps to this book—proves once again that being a bit "salty" is exactly what the world wants and needs? Maybe our culture has an appetite for meat and not milk, for strong wine rather than weak, for the dangers of rushing rivers rather than the safety of calm stagnant ponds? Could it be the world, more so than the Church, realizes that if we are ever going to get out of the mess we've created for ourselves and for those generations that follow, we need a university and not a day care?

Instead of taking a stand, many allegedly Christian school leaders change Scripture to appear more accepting of new ideas. I talk with a lot of university leaders, many of whom tell me in confidence they would like to be more bold and forthright, but their faculty attack them when they do. I know several peers, i.e. leaders in Christian higher education, who say they completely understand my exasperation and in fact privately share it. They want to do the right thing, but they know they will face faculty opposition and lack of support from their board. They know their sponsoring church may not want to take a stand.

While I don't agree with their silence, I do admit I understand why so few speak out—fear. Fear of a vote of *no confidence* from the liberal faculty. Fear the board will capitulate to public pressure. Fear the parents will complain. Fear of a Church that seems more interested in being politically correct than in doing what is morally right. Fear of an academic culture that resists strong leadership and punishes it more often than it rewards it. I once heard a faculty member at one of these universities state dismissively, "Presidents come and presidents go, but I stay." In his mind, he and his fellow faculty were in charge and the college president was irrelevant and, frankly, somewhat unwelcome. It's sad to say, but in many cases he is absolutely correct. As you watch the snowflake rebellion play out on campuses across the nation ask yourself this: Have university presidents indeed become essentially irrelevant? Do you see strength or weakness in their leadership? Do they show any evidence that they have the convictions to stand in the face of this nonsense or does your gut tell you that they are simply more concerned with keeping their job? Or even worse, do they seem to actually believe that giving Play Doh, bubbles, and coloring books to a bunch of twenty-year-olds who don't like the results of an election is a good idea?

THE EVANGELICAL MODEL

What is the evangelical Christian university? What should it be? What must it be? These are the questions that have consumed much of my professional life for the past three decades in my various roles as a dean and vice president and now president within the community of universities that claim to be "Christ-centered," "evangelical," and "Christian." In fact, I chose this topic for my doctoral dissertation at Michigan State University. My goal in my research was to understand and highlight what students, parents, pastors, alumni, faculty, and staff believe we mean when we use *evangelical* and *Christian* to define and describe a college or university.

My bias in my research was clear: Christian colleges must be honest and direct about what it means to be *evangelical* and *Christian* in our methods, mission, and mores. We must understand what our defining adjectives mean to our various constituents. We must work to fulfill the expectations that these descriptors raise in the minds of our students, parents, pastors, alumni, faculty, staff, and board. To do otherwise compromises our own integrity and the integrity of the university and its mission. To do otherwise falls short of accreditation standards. To do otherwise borders on dishonesty—dishonesty in our advertising, marketing, recruiting, and teaching—and it causes confusion and implies mediocrity. We cannot be all things to all people and any organization, team, church, college, or university gets caught in a melancholy quagmire when it attempts to be so.

My assumption (in my research and in my practice) is our constituents believe an evangelical worldview is unique and exceptional and these students, parents, and pastors, etc. expect us to "measure up." My contention is when we are faithful to an evangelical ethos and biblical worldview, our constituents are encouraged and excited, but when we are not, they become complacent, confused, and lose trust.

Our mission and vision must have integrity and be grounded in the pursuit of truth—all truth. This should not only be the mission embraced by Oklahoma Wesleyan University, it should be the mission embraced by schools across the country—to be passionate and totally given to the proposition that all truth is God's truth.

As I've told our faculty and staff at Oklahoma Wesleyan, we attract students to our campus because of the intuitive "fit" they feel between the truth for which they hunger and our promise of helping them pursue that truth as the ultimate measure for all learning and all living. My own research has confirmed this and my personal experience in higher education has likewise shown repeatedly that our constituents are attracted to and excited about an evangelical university because of this "fit." They expect us to honor a specific definition of what man is for, what community is about, who God is, and how truth will be pursued and judged.

I firmly believe success follows those who share a clear definition, bold direction, and dynamic cause. Our success at Oklahoma Wesleyan University is clear proof of that truth. A biblical, evangelical, Christian worldview that honors the Lordship of Jesus Christ in all ways and at all times is the bedrock of such success. The president, faculty, and staff of any Christian college or university should make—indeed, *must* make—such clarity and boldness their guiding priority and the foundation of any vision.

I contend an evangelical Christian university is, by definition, one that models a way of thought, a way of life, and a way of faith. This does not mean schools like Oklahoma Wesleyan are places of thoughtless indoctrination. To the contrary, they are places of serious study, honest questions, and critical engagement, all in the context of humble allegiance to the traditions and teachings of the evangelical (and in our case the Wesleyan) Church. John Piper offers this superb summary of what the Christian university should be:

> Indoctrination is not the only alternative to faith-weakening education. In our day, the word "indoctrination" usually refers to the unthinking transmission of tradition. But I would affirm strongly that this is not the only alternative.... The real alternative is a

faculty made up of great Christian thinkers who are great lovers of God with profound allegiance to the truth of God's Word and razor-sharp discernment of all the subtle idols of our age. What is needed is great teachers with great hearts for the great old verities of the faith—verities that they hold because there are great reasons for holding them—reasons that will stand up to hard questions.... Our problem is not that "indoctrination" is the only alternative to education. It isn't. Our problem is that so few have ever tasted great Christian education or seen great Christian thinking going on from a profoundly God-centered perspective in an atmosphere where students can feel that the faculty would gladly die for Jesus.[2]

As Christians, we must have a clear mission (i.e. our duty, our purpose) with clear "cornerstones" that serve as our indispensable foundation. I believe these absolute tenets should be the *priority of Scripture* as the context for seeking all wisdom and knowledge; the *pursuit of truth* as the objective goal for students wishing to develop critical minds and discerning spirits; the *primacy of Jesus Christ* as our Lord who is the alpha and omega, the beginning and the end of all learning and all living; and the *practice of wisdom*, holy living by which all members of this community (faculty, staff, students, board members, and alumni, etc.) promote healing and wholeness in a broken culture and hurting world.

IT IS TIME

The foremost priority for any Christian college should be excellence and integrity within the context of a community where "Great Christian thinking goes on from a profoundly God-centered perspective in an atmosphere where students feel that the faculty would gladly die for Jesus." Such a focus is not optional. We must not and cannot afford to fail. This is our time.

It is time for us to show our students and our community there is an objective measure for life, for morality, for truthfulness, integrity, and honesty.

It is time for us to boldly enter the "town square" and practice wisdom by "doing justice, loving mercy and walking humbly with our God"(Micah 6:8).

It is time for us to "let our light so shine before men that they may see our good works and give praise to our Father in heaven"(Matthew 5:16).

It is time for us to be ready to "give an answer"—a well-reasoned and sound *apologia* for our faith, our values, and our way of life.

It is time for us acknowledge before our peers that the "Lord is God" and He "teaches what is best" and "directs in the way [we] should go" and the "fear of the Lord is the beginning of Wisdom" (Proverbs 9:10).

It is time for us to teach our younger students to "remember [their] Creator in the days of their youth" and for our older students to "remember him before the silver cord is broken"(Ecclesiastes 12:6).

It is time for all of us to remember "of making of many books there is no end, and much study wearies the body" and "everything is meaningless" unless we "fear God and keep his commandments for this is the whole duty of man" (Ecclesiastes 12:13).

This is the time for evangelical Christian leaders to lead "universities where Jesus is Lord" and to be a people who boldly pursue truth—God's truth—in everything we do as we reclaim every inch of creation for Christ and His Kingdom.

This is what makes us *evangelical* and *Christian*. This is what makes us worthwhile to our students and to each other. This is what brings God's favor and blessing. This is what makes us a university and not a day care.

MY PRAYER

This is a prayer of confession that I delivered recently in Oklahoma City at National Day of Prayer event and then again at the opening of the state's GOP convention in 2017. I offer it again here. I offer it with a sober spirit and contrite heart. My profession, education, has failed our culture and its children. It is my hope that many professors in the halls of academe and many parents in the homes across America will join me, not just today, but continually as we seek God's forgiveness and repent of what we have done to our kids and our culture.

God, you have told us that if your people will humble themselves and seek your face and repent that you will hear us and heal us. You have also told us that if we confess our sins that you are faithful and just and that you will forgive our sins and cleanse us from all unrighteousness. God we bow before you today. We are humble. We repent. Please hear our prayer. Please, forgive us...

Forgive us for what we have taught our children.

Forgive us for teaching them that evil is good and good is evil, that darkness is light and light is darkness, that bitter is sweet and sweet is bitter. Forgive us for teaching them that left is right and right is wrong, that true is false and falsehood is true.

Forgive us for teaching them that a career is more important than character, money is more important than morality, and information is more important than integrity.

Forgive us, Holy God, for teaching sexual promiscuity in our schools more effectively than we have taught sexual restraint to our students. Forgive us for teaching self-esteem better than we have taught science and civics. Forgive us for teaching values clarification more than virtue. Forgive us for diminishing the value of marital fidelity and leaving our kids clueless as to how to defend the definition of marriage.

Forgive us for teaching the generation that follows us to believe it has the authority to define life for the generation that follows it. Forgive us for teaching them that "choice" gives them the power to take away the right of the weakest to choose.

Forgive us for our narcissism: for proclaiming we are "as God"; that "we are the ones we've been waiting for and that we are the change we seek."

Forgive us for making justice unjust and injustice just.

Forgive us for celebrating lies rather than pursuing truth.

Forgive us for our self-refuting duplicity of pedantically preaching that the tolerant do not tolerate those they find intolerable.

Forgive us for the hypocrisy of hating those we find hateful.

Forgive us for diminishing human dignity and for dumbing down the definition of the *imago Dei* to the imago dog; for diminishing human identity to little more than the sum total of our base inclinations, appetites, proclivities, passions, feelings, and desires.

Forgive us for pretending that women should not be subjected to the power and passions of men but then electing men who subject women to their delusional and dysphoric passions.

Forgive us, God, for teaching young men to view young women as nothing but objects of recreation. Forgive us for teaching our young women to accept this insult to their dignity.

Forgive us for boasting of freedom while yet living in bondage to our own deception.

Forgive us for separating head from heart and fact from faith.

Forgive us for severing belief from behavior and religion from reason.

Forgive us for "removing the organ and demanding the function"—for creating "men without chests"—for the foolishness of "gelding the stallion and bidding him be fruitful."

Forgive us for confusing liberty with license and freedom with fascism.

Forgive us for teaching our children to worship government more than God and to trust in Caesar more than Christ.

God, we ask you to forgive us for what we have taught our children. We ask that you rescue them from the ugly hell of our own making. We humbly petition you to grant a reprieve of your judgment. We ask that you rescue them from the bondage of our arrogance and pride.

Please save our kids, oh Lord, from our lies and grant them freedom in your Truth. In the name of Jesus Christ, the Way, the Truth, and the Life, we pray: please forgive us for what we have taught our children.

Amen and Amen.

CONCLUSION: THE UNITY OF FIRST THINGS

"**I**f fascism ever comes to America," Ronald Reagan told Mike Wallace in 1975, "it will come in the name of liberalism." Indeed, ideological fascism has come in place of academic freedom, waiving the banners of *trigger warnings*, *microaggressions*, and *safe spaces* on college campuses across the land. You must submit. You must agree. You must comply with the *fasces*—the acceptable bundle of ideas—or or you will be silenced and expelled.

C. S. Lewis told us in *God in the Dock*: "Put first things first and second things are thrown in. Put second things first and you lose both first and second things."[1] In his publication titled *First Things* John Richard Neuhaus told us, "One must never underestimate the profound bigotry and anti-intellectualism and intolerance and illiberality of liberalism."[2]

The Academy should be about first things, not second things. It should be about an exceptional curriculum rather than the common core. It should be more concerned with ethics than information, and character more than careers. It should focus on how to acquire morality more so than merely earning more money. The truly educated person should be dedicated to pursuing truth not constructing opinions, and embracing love rather than simply being tolerant. Good education should be about *first things*, and not be content with those that are second. To paraphrase Lewis again: when we can have a holiday at the beach, why in the world are we satisfied with making mud pies in the back alleys?

College life should be about promoting unity, not division. It's called a "uni-versity" and not a "di-versity" for a reason. Classical education—truly *liberating* education—is about the common cause of personal righteousness, not the divisiveness of our personal rights. Selflessness rather than self. The *unum* rather than the *pluribus*. *Veritas* and *virtue* rather than vindication and vengeance. It's about pursuing what's *good*, rather than being satisfied with what seems *safe*.

As Lewis says, when we reverse the order and focus on second things we get neither first nor second. It is only by dying to self that any human being will ever find his true identity. It isn't found in race or gender. It isn't found in personal grievances or our narcissistic infatuation with self. We are neither Jew nor Greek, male nor female, slave nor free. We are human beings, and selfless unity in Christ is the First Thing.

Professors, politicians, pundits and, yes, even parents do our next generation of leaders and consequently our country great harm by enabling young people to miss the *first things* by fixating on the second things. As Neuhaus warned, such ontological dyslexia brings only "profound bigotry and anti-intellectualism and intolerance and illiberality of liberalism." It brings cries of "microaggressions" and calls for "trigger warnings." It runs *from* the debate rather than *toward* it. It brings exclusion rather than inclusion, and segregation rather than integration.

This was the genius of William Wilberforce. His "am I not a man" campaign focused on the unity of what it meant to be a human being, not on the division of what it meant to be of a given race or gender or social status. By focusing on unity and not division, he forced the British culture to deal with the First Thing: the dignity of all men and women, rather than let them get distracted by the sins of resistance, retrenchment, or revenge.

In the cover story of the April 2017 issue of *Christianity Today*, Mark Galli makes this point well:

> The problem with [identity politics] goes even deeper than disunity. It encourages me [and others] to notice what is passing away while failing to notice the reality of what will last....
>
> Given human nature, [a fixation on] identity...seems to inevitably degenerate into judgmentalism and division. Identity based on common interest, experience, or even conviction [gender or race] cannot enable the one thing that Jesus is most eager for us to do: Come together in unity in him.
>
> The fixation on diversity... has produced a generation of liberals and progressives narcissistically unaware of conditions outside their self-defined groups.... Identity liberalism has failed... National politics in healthy periods is not about 'differences'; it is about commonality....

> As we keep reading the New Testament faithfully,
> this reality sinks into us more and more deeply. As
> much as we take pride in our social, economic, gen-
> der...and many other differences, we'll keep coming
> back to the most amazing thing about each of us: We
> have died with Christ and it is not we who live (with
> those various identities...we're so proud of) but
> Christ who lives in us. That's our glory. That's our
> identity.[3]

Over the past thirty years, I have had at least fifteen different college students live with my family. These students became part of our family while they attended college. The majority of these kids were from different cultures and some were even from other countries. In my house, unity, not diversity, has been our concern. We are family, pure and simple. We see character, not color, age, nationality or social status. We celebrate what we have in common and don't worry about how we differ. We focus on the Savior and not the self. We hold each other accountable to righteousness and don't defend our rights.

My family's identity is in Christ, not in individual grievances. Everyone under my roof "is a man," nothing more and nothing less. There are no subdivisions. My home is a uni-versity. It is not a di-versity. It is a place where everyone is expected to act like an adult and not behave like a child. It is not a day care.

I was recently asked if, by espousing the views I have expressed in this book, I was trying to "force unity" on the more broadly diverse subcategories of our culture. It was inferred that I was, thereby, ignoring the the disenfranchised and those who stand on the fringes and in the shadows of American society. I responded by asking this question: Is it possible that the best way to support the disadvantaged and underprivileged is to embrace unity rather than promote division and to welcome everyone into the family of Americans without hyphenating their identity? I would argue that what my challenger implied would be more accurately defined as *compliance*, not unity. I would also contend that the irony was that he, as a progressive, was the one demanding compliance with his standards, his rules, and his legalism while I, as the conservative, was the one arguing for unity and its implied foundation of liberty. Forced unity is an oxymoron—if it's forced, it's not unity. Compliance, however *is* forced. There is a huge difference between the conservative's fight for unity and the progressive's attempt to force everyone else to comply. One is freedom, while one is fascism. One celebrates the whole, while one condemns those who are not part of the group. One confronts, while one coddles. One thrives by rule of love, while one exists by the tyranny of the gang. One produces mature adults, the other produces self-absorbed snowflakes.

A PERSONAL NOTE FOR AMERICA

As I was working on this book, my younger brother called me with a sobering story. His eighteen-year-old son was a mess. Meth, marijuana, alcohol, lying, theft—all of it led my nephew to jail. My brother called me, broken-hearted, asking me what to do.

My response: leave him there. Don't bail him out. He needs to wake up to reality and suffer the consequences for his bad ideas, bad decisions, and bad behavior. If you keep rescuing him, I told his father, he will feel artificially safe in his sin and dysfunction. He'll never have any reason to change. He'll never grow up, if you keep coddling him.

My brother actually followed my advice and did the hard, but loving thing. He told his son, because he did love him, he was not going to enable him any longer. He was going to let the crisis play out with the hope and prayer his son would finally come to his senses and become a man of character rather than a characterless man.

This morning as I edited the final chapters of this book, my brother called and put his son on the phone. My nephew proceeded to tell me he was drug free, sober, and working a steady job at a local ski resort. He stopped doing all the things that got him in so much trouble in the past.

I told my nephew I was proud of him and then asked: "I'm just curious, what happened that caused the change?" His response should be a lesson to every American: "I needed to hit rock bottom and I finally did."

It was my brother's loving courage to confront that created a solid "rock bottom" upon which his son could firmly plant his feet, grow up, and become a man. The previous coddling did nothing but cripple his development by perpetuating the illusion of a "safe space" of prolonged immaturity and rebellious adolescence.

My brother and my nephew now clearly understand and embody the main point of this book. The reality is that life, like education, is never safe, but it can be good. Our colleges, universities, families, churches, and our entire nation desperately need to learn the same lesson if we are to continue to live free and thrive.

After all, this not a day care. This is America.

ACKNOWLEDGMENTS

Special thanks are due to many who have stood shoulder to shoulder with me in the fight for academic freedom and intellectual liberty. Key mentors as well as trusted partners are always as important as the point man himself when fighting the good fight for what is right and just and true. I am grateful for those who have helped me find clarity when I needed it, precision where I lacked it, and conviction where I avoided it.

In this context, I am humbled by the complementary nature of the broader body of Christ. Some obviously have clearer eyes and keener ears to see what needs to be seen and to hear what needs to be heard a bit sooner than the rest of us. While there are many godly men and women whom I should thank and affirm, I would be remiss not to mention the following few.

Chuck Colson was a great hero of common sense and of Christian integrity. His Christian conversion and subsequent defense of the Faith and the truth that undergirds it is perhaps one of God's greatest gifts to our country and to the Church in the past fifty years. Dr. Colson truly modeled what it meant to be born again and to thereby be salt and light to a dying culture and an increasingly dark and hurting world.

Dr. Jim Garlow continues to be a great friend and courageous confidant. I know of few who I would trust more to stand shoulder to shoulder with me in the battle for ideas and the defense of truth. He is one of the most articulate spokesmen I know for the cause of Christ.

I am forever grateful for the privilege of studying under the likes of Os Guinness, John Lennox, and the other professors at the Oxford Center for Christian Apologetics. What a gift to be able to learn from their teaching and be inspired by their leadership.

I am honored and humbled by the inexplicable loyalty and support of Josh McDowell. Josh is the poster child of what it means to be a brother in Christ. If you Google the words "true friend" the first thing that you will see pop up on your screen is a picture of Josh McDowell.

Governor Frank Keating is another exemplary leader who has blessed me with his confidence, inspired me with his courage, and emboldened me with his praise.

Audrea Taylor contributed greatly to this book. She stitched together many speeches, radio commentaries, editorials, and opinion pieces, to create broader, more cohesive arguments.

Rick Borman has likewise provided untold hours of counsel and insight in navigating the waters of public relations, publications, radio, TV, and the Internet. Without Rick, I am not sure how we would have weathered the "Not a Day Care" storm without drowning in its flood.

Roger Metcalf, Steve Babby, Don Walker, Trevor Shakiba, Kevin Freeman, Marla Roseland, Gale Kane, and the rest of the Oklahoma Board of Trustees deserve a special note of thanks for graciously granting me the time to engage in the "extracurricular activities" necessary to complete this book.

Bill Blankschaen deserves a special note of thanks for his role as co-writer. His assistance in research, writing, and editing all proved incredibly valuable. He and I both know the end product would not have been as solid without his partnership.

Finally, there is no one in the list above who even comes close to holding a candle to my wife, Marci. She is the most faithful follower of Christ I know. Every day Marci models for my two sons and for me what conviction, courage, forgiveness, and faithfulness really means. My family is blessed beyond words to have her as its matriarch.

NOTES

1: CRYING OURSELVES TO DEATH

1. The Pitt Maverick, "Pitt students take to streets after Trump victory," Campusreform.org, November 9, 2016, http://www.campusreform.org/?ID=8362.
2. Anthony Gockowski, "Profs cancel classes to 'cope' with 'anxiety and terror' of Trump win," Campusreform.org, November 9, 2016, http://www.campusreform.org/?ID=8365.
3. DailyMail.com reporter, "Outrage as California professor is filmed telling students that Trump is a 'white supremacist' whose election was an 'act of terrorism,'" *Daily Mail*, December 9, 2016, http://www.dailymail.co.uk/news/article-4017786/Professor-draws-ire-telling-students-Donald-Trump-s-election-act-terrorism-president-elect-white-supremacist.html#ixzz4SRLv4G7R.

4. Anthony Gockowski, "Berkeley student assaulted for MAGA hat one day after riots," Campusreform.org, February 3, 2017, https://www.campusreform.org/?ID=8733.

5. Anthony Gockowski,"Only one arrest, at most, made at Berkeley protest," Campusreform.org, February 2, 2017, https://www.campusreform.org/?ID=8726.

6. Emily Marks, "Free Speech in College: University's Rejection of Conservative Club Ignites Debate," *University Herald*, February 20, 2017, http://www.universityherald.com/articles/65999/20170220/free-speech-college-university-rejection-conservative-club-ignites-debate.htm.

7. Jillian Kay Melchior, "Muzzled Professors: An Inside Look at How One College Lets Students Censor Classroom Debate," *HeatStreet*, June 19, 2016, https://heatst.com/culture-wars/an-inside-look-at-how-one-college-is-censoring-classroom-debate/.

8. Todd Starnes, "Town Hall Mob Explodes at the Name of Jesus," Toddstarnes.com, February 26, 2017, https://www.toddstarnes.com/column/town-hall-mob-explodes-at-the-name-of-jesus.

9. Todd Beamon, "NYC Releases List of 31 Genders: Man, Woman, 'Something Else Entirely,'" *NewsMax*, June 1, 2016, http://www.newsmax.com/Newsfront/NYC-releases-gender-list/2016/06/01/id/731809/.

10. RT Question More, "University of London students demand 'white philosophers' like Plato, Kant removed from syllabus," *RT*, January 9, 2017, https://www.rt.com/uk/373042-white-philosophers-students-demand/.

11. John Etchemendy, "John Etchemendy: 'The threat from within,'" Stanford News, February 21, 2017, http://news.stanford.edu/2017/02/21/the-threat-from-within/.

2: THE SNOWFLAKE INSANITY

1. Elliot Dordick, "Scripps College: Nonwhite Students Should be Paid for Sharing Their Opinions," *Claremont Independent*, February 28, 2017, http://claremontindependent.com/scripps-college-nonwhite-students-should-be-paid-for-sharing-their-opinions/.

2. Becca Stanek, "Oberlin students want to abolish midterms and any grades below C," *The Week*, May 25, 2016, http://theweek.com/speedreads/626361/oberlin-students-want-abolish-midterms-grades-below-c.

3. Nathan Heller, "The Big Uneasy—What's roiling the liberal-arts campus?" *The New Yorker*, May 30, 2016, http://www.newyorker.com/magazine/2016/05/30/the-new-activism-of-liberal-arts-colleges.

4. "Middlebury College professor injured by protesters as she escorted controversial speaker," *Addison County Independent*, March 6, 2017, http://www.addisonindependent.com/201703middlebury-college-professor-injured-protesters-she-escorted-controversial-speaker.

5. Lukas Mikelionis, "Left-Wing Berkeley Protesters Demand 'Spaces of Color', Harass White Students Trying to Pass," *HeatStreet*, October 24, 2016, https://heatst.com/culture-wars/left-wing-berkeley-protesters-demand-spaces-of-color-harass-white-students-trying-to-pass/.

6. Douglas Ernst, "Notre Dame students 'feel unsafe' about Pence invite, start protest campaign," *Washington Times*, April 11, 2017, http://www.washingtontimes.com/news/2017/apr/11/notre-dame-students-feel-unsafe-about-mike-pence-i/

7. Chris Perez, and Gina Diadone, "Protesters storm NYU over conservative speaker's seminar," *New York Post*, February 2,

2017, http://nypost.com/2017/02/02/protesters-storm-nyu-over-conservative-speakers-seminar/.

8. Diana Valentine, "Liberal College Students' War on Chick-fil-A Continues," *The National Pulse*, April 11, 2017, https://thenationalpulse.com/culture/liberal-college-students-declare-war-chick-fil-a/.

9. David French, "A Suicide in Texas," *National Review*, April 12, 2017, http://www.nationalreview.com/node/446681/print[4/13/2017.

10. Judith Shulevitz, "In College and Hiding From Scary Idea," *The New York Times*, March 21, 2015, https://www.nytimes.com/2015/03/22/opinion/sunday/judith-shulevitz-hiding-from-scary-ideas.html?_r=1.

11. Mason Clark, "UMich students demand no-whites-allowed space to plot 'social justice' activism," *The College Fix*, February 23, 2017, http://www.thecollegefix.com/post/31322/.

12. Kate Hardiman, "UW-Madison's Young Americans for Freedom labeled hate group," *The College Fix*, January 6, 2017, http://www.thecollegefix.com/post/30609.

13. Michael Cantrell, "OUTRAGEOUS: University hosts most PATHETIC post-inaugural event featuring…" *Allen B. West*, January 25, 2017, http://www.allenbwest.com/michaelcantrell/outrageous-university-hosts-pathetic-post-inaugural-event-featuring.

14. Anthony Gockowski, "AU students retreat to 'stress free zone' for cocoa, corn hole," *Campus Reform*, December 9, 2016, http://www.campusleadership.org/?ID=8513.

15. Jonathan Petre, "They Kant be serious! PC students demand white philosophers including Plato and Descartes be dropped from university syllabus," *Daily Mail*, January 7, 2017, "http://www.dailymail.co.uk/news/article-4098332/They-Kant-PC-students-demand-white

-philosophers-including-Plato-Descartes-dropped-university-syllabus.
html.

16. Adam Steinbaugh, "Hundreds of campuses encourage students to turn in fellow students for offensive speech," *Washington Examiner*, February 21, 2017, http://www.washingtonexaminer. com/hundreds-of-campuses-encourage-students-to-turn-in-fellow-students-for-offensive-speech/article/2615405#.WK2cLEhVcPs. facebook.

3: I'LL BET YOU THINK LIFE IS ABOUT YOU

1. William & Mary Events Calendar, "[Past Event] Thanksgiving Toolkit: How to Handle Politically-Motivated Family Conflict and Take Care of Yourself," William & Mary, November 21, 2016, https://events.wm.edu/event/view/wm/81400.

2. Joey Ye, "Silliman associate master's Halloween email draws ire," *Yale Daily News*, November 2, 2015, http://yaledailynews.com/ blog/2015/11/02/silicon-associate-masters-halloween-email-draws-ire/.

3. Ibid.

4. Joel Stein, "Millennials: The Me Me Me Generation," *Time*, May 20, 2013, http://time.com/247/millennials-the-me-me-me-generation/ .

5. Emily Ekins, "65% of Americans Say Millennials Are 'Entitled,' 58% of Millennials Agree," Reason.com., August 19, 2014, http:// reason.com/poll/2014/08/19/65-of-americans-say-millennials-are-enti.

6. Emma Miller, "Pew survey: Millennials are crazy critical of Millennial generation," *USA Today College*, September 15, 2015, http://college.usatoday.com/2015/09/15/millennial-generation-pew-survey-podcast/.

7. Joseph Erbentraut, "Here's More Proof That Millennials Are the 'Giving Generation,'" *The Huffington Post,* December 1, 2015, http://www.huffingtonpost.com/2015/07/08/millennial-donations-to-charity_n_7739736.html.

8. Jay Gilbert, "The Millennials: A new generation of employees, a new set of engagement policies," *Ivy Business Journal,* September/October 2011, http://iveybusinessjournal.com/publication/the-millennials-a-new-generation-of-employees-a-new-set-of-engagement-policies/.

4: PRO-WOMAN—AND PROUD OF IT!

1. Ruth Padawer, "When Women Become Men at Wellesley," *The New York Times,* October 15, 2014, https://www.nytimes.com/2014/10/19/magazine/when-women-become-men-at-wellesley-college.html.

2. "About the NAIA," National Association of Intercollegiate Athletics, http://www.naia.org/ViewArticle.dbml?DB_OEM_ID=27900&ATCLID=205323019.

3. Samuel Smith,"Alabama University Gives Men Access to Girls' Bathrooms to Comply With Obama's Transgender Rules," *The Christian Post*, August 12, 2016, http://www.christianpost.com/news/alabama-university-gives-men-access-girls-bathrooms-comply-obamas-transgender-rules-167894/.

4. Barbara Hollingsworth,"University of Iowa to Use 'Preferred Pronouns' When Addressing Students," *CNS News,* July 22, 2016, http://www.cnsnews.com/news/article/barbara-hollingsworth/university-iowa-use-preferred-pronouns-when-addressing-students.

5. Nahema Marchal, "Michigan student successfully changes preferred pronoun to 'His Majesty' on class roster," *Fox News*, September 30, 2016, http://www.foxnews.com/us/2016/09/30/

michigan-student-successfully-changes-preferred-pronoun-to-his-majesty-on-class-roster.html.

5: CORRUPTED AND COMPROMISING CHRISTIAN UNIVERSITIES

1. Emily Jashinsky, "Samford Blocks YAF Chapter for 'Inflammatory' Sharon Statement," Young America's Foundation, November 29, 2016, http://www.yaf.org/news/samford-blocks-yaf/.

2. Jennifer Kabbany, "Christian university to send students to mosque for 'religious experience,'" The College Fix, January 24, 2017, http://www.thecollegefix.com/post/30861/.

3. Rob Shimshock, "School Celebrates Valentine's Day with No Classes and Lots of Social Justice," Daily Caller, February 15, 2017, http://dailycaller.com/2017/02/15/christian-college-cancels-class-for-social-justice-workshop/.

4. Nathan Rubbelke, "Students demand Catholic univerity denounce Saint Junipero Serra as mass murderer," The College Fix, December 23, 2015, http://www.thecollegefix.com/post/25614/.

6: IDEAS HAVE CONSEQUENCES

1. Tribune News Services. "Ohio State attacker was angry about treatment of Muslims, official says," Chicago Tribune, November 29, 2016, http://www.chicagotribune.com/news/nationworld/ct-ohio-state-campus-attack-20161129-story.html.

2. Amanda Tidwell, "After Ohio State students attacked by radical Muslim, campus hosts 'Islamophobia' talk," The College Fix, February 18, 2017, http://www.thecollegefix.com/post/31262/.

3. The Ohio State University: Middle East Studies Center, "Islamophobia: Its causes and consequences, how to counter it in daily life," February 20, 2017, https://mesc.osu.edu/events/islamophobia-its-causes-and-consequences.

4. Elizabeth Suarez, "Abdul Razak Ali Artan's name added to student group's list of people of color killed by police," *The Lantern*, December 8, 2016, http://thelantern.com/2016/12/abdul-razak-ali-artans-name-added-to-student-groups-list-of-people-of-color-killed-by-police/.

5. Bradford Richardson, "Ohio State University attacker was enrolled in class studying 'microaggressions,'" *The Washington Times*, December 1, 2016, http://www.washingtontimes.com/news/2016/dec/1/abdul-razak-ali-artan-ohio-state-university-attack/.

6. C. S. Lewis, *That Hideous Strength* (London: Harper Collins, 2001).

7. Charles W. Colson and Nancy Pearcey, *How Now Shall We Live?* (Carol Stream, IL: Tyndale House Publishers, Incorporated, 2011), 92.

8. Colson and Pearcey, 93.

9. T. S. Eliot, "The Aims of Education," lecture given at the University of Chicago, 1950.

10. Colson and Pearcey, 187.

11. Jason Howerton, "Obama on 'Twisted' Islamic State Views: 'Ideologies Are Not Defeated with Guns, They Are Defeated With Better Ideas,'" *The Blaze*, July 6, 2015, http://www.theblaze.com/stories/2015/07/06/obama-on-islamic-state-ideologies-are-not-defeated-with-guns-they-are-defeated-with-better-ideas/.

12. "Professors Ranked Best for Third Year in a Row," Oklahoma Wesleyan University, http://www.okwu.edu/blog/2013/02/professors/; Lynn O'Shaughnessy, "25 Colleges with the Best Professors," *CBS Money Watch*, December 1, 2010, http://www.cbsnews.com/news/25-colleges-with-the-best-professors/.

7: THE PRODIGAL UNIVERSITY

1. Kate Hardiman, "University of Missouri implements mandatory 'diversity and inclusion training,'" *The College Fix*, October 13, 205, http://www.thecollegefix.com/post/24609/.

2. W. Ringenberg, *The Christian College: A History of Protestant Higher Education in America* (Grand Rapids, MI: Christian University Press, 1984).

3. J. D. Hunter, *Evangelicalism: The Coming Generation* (Chicago: University of Chicago Press, 1987), 166.

4. Ringenberg, *The Christian College*, 3–9.

5. Hunter, *Evangelicalism: The Coming Generation*, 166.

6. Ibid., 165.

7. Harvard GSAS Christian Community, "Shield and 'Veritas' History," http://www.hcs.harvard.edu/~gsascf/shield-and-veritas-history/.

8. Edwin Oviatt, *The Beginnings of Yale (1701–1726)* (New Haven: Yale University Press, 1916).

9. Society for the Promotion of Collegiate and Theological Education at the West, *Permanent Documents of the Society for the Promotion of Collegiate and Theological Education at the West*, vol. 1 (Nabu Press, 2010), 30.

10. "Dartmouth at a Glance," Dartmouth website, http://dartmouth.edu/dartmouth-glance.

11. University of Pennsylvania, "Frequently Asked Questions," https://secure.www.upenn.edu/secretary/FAQ.html.

12. Brown University "From Martha Mitchell's *Encyclopedia Brunoniana*," Office of University Communications, http://www.brown.edu/Administration/News_Bureau/Databases/Encyclopedia/search.php?serial=S0090.

13. Columbia University, "History," http://www.columbia.edu/content/history-identity.html.

14. Hunter, *Evangelicalism: The Coming Generation*, 167.

15. Ibid.

16. Reed G. Geiger, *Planning the French Canals*: *Bureaucracy, Politics, and Enterprise Under the Restoration* (Newark: University of Delaware Press, 1994), 18.

17. Ibid., 19.

18. Kassy Dillon, "After protests and riots, free speech is MIA on college campuses," *The Hill*, February 23, 2017, http://thehill.com/blogs/pundits-blog/education/317719-after-protests-and-riots-free-speech-is-mia-on-college-campuses.

8: THE INTOLERANCE OF THE TOLERANT LEFT

1. C. S. Lewis, *The Lion, the Witch and the Wardrobe* (New York: Scholastic, 1995).

2. Lewis, *Mere Christianity* (London: Collins, 2012).

3. Benjamin Wood,"University of Utah removes references to anti-LGBT groups from bio of honorary degree recipient," *The Salt Lake Tribune*, April 28, 2016, http://www.sltrib.com/home/3827168-155/university-of-utah-removes-references-to.

4. Jordan B. Peterson, *Maps of Meaning*: *The Architecture of Belief* (New York: Routledge, 1999).

5. Jason Tucker and Jason VandenBeukel,"'We're teaching university students lies' –An interview with Dr. Jordan Peterson," *C2C Journal*, December 1, 2016, http://www.c2cjournal.ca/2016/12/were-teaching-university-students-lies-an-interview-with-dr-jordan-peterson/.

6. Harvey A. Silverglate, David French, and Greg Lukianoff,"Free Speech Rights on Private College Campuses," Know My Rights, http://www.knowmyrights.org/index.php?option=com_

content&view=article&id=44:free-speech-rights-on-private-colle
gecampuses&catid=18&Itemid=123&showall=1&limitstart.

7. Rachel Percelay,"Here's Why the World Congress of Families Conference is so Scary," *The Advocate*, October 30, 2015, http:// www.advocate.com/commentary/2015/10/30/heres-why-world-congress-families-conference-so-scary.

8. Andrew Sullivan,"Is Intersectionality a Religion?" *New York Magazine*, March 10, 2017, http://nymag.com/daily/ intelligencer/2017/03/is-intersectionality-a-religion.html.

9. C. S. Lewis, "The Poison of Subjectivism," in *Christian Reflections* (Grand Rapids: Eerdmans, 1967).

9: DO WE REALLY TRUST OURSELVES?

1. Billy Preston, "Nothing from Nothing," Universal Music Publishing Group, http://www.metrolyrics.com/nothing-from-nothing-lyrics-billy-preston.html.

2. Shirley Jackson, *The Lottery and Other Stories*; *The Haunting of Hill House*; *We Have Always Lived in the Castle* (New York: Quality Paperback Book Club, 1991).

3. Kay Haugaard, "Students Who Won't Decry Evil—a Case of Too Much Tolerance?" *The Chronicle of Higher Education*, June 27, 1997, http://www.chronicle.com/article/Students-Who-Wont-Decry-Evil/74720.

4. Ibid.

5. Shirley Jackson and Os Guinness, ed., "The Lottery," and Kay Hauggard, "The Lottery Revisited," in *Unriddling Our Times*: *Reflections on the Gathering Cultural Crisis* (Grand Rapids, MI: Baker Books, 1999), 123–141.

10: OUR CULTURAL AVERSION TO ADVERSITY

1. George W. Rutler, "A Populist Election and Its Aftermath," *Crisis*, November 17, 2016, http://www.crisismagazine.com/2016/populist-election-aftermath.

2. C. S. Lewis, *The Silver Chair* (New York: Scholastic Inc., 1987).

3. Carl Sagan, *Cosmos* (New York: Random House Inc., 2002).

4. Sam LaGrone, "Navy to Name Ship After Gay Rights Activist Harvey Milk," USNI News, July 28, 2016, https://news.usni.org/2016/07/28/navy-name-ship-gay-rights-activist-harvey-milk.

5. Victor Stenger, "The Rising Antiscience," The *Huffington Post*, September 27, 2013, http://www.huffingtonpost.com/victor-stenger/rising-antiscience-faith_b_3991677.html.

6. Colson and Pearcey, *How Now Shall We Live? Study Guide*, 243.

11: OUR EDUCATION NIGHTMARE

1. Walter E. Williams, "On Education, the Left Protects a Miserable Status Quo," *The Daily Signal*, March 1, 2017, http://dailysignal.com/2017/03/01/on-education-the-left-protects-a-miserable-status-quo/.

2. C. S. Lewis, *Mere Christianity* (London: Collins, 2012).

3. "Letter From a Birmingham Jail," Stanford—The Martin Luther King, Jr. Research and Education Institute, https://kinginstitute.stanford.edu/king-papers/documents/letter-birmingham-jail.

4. Heather Long, "Conservatives aren't welcome in New York, according to Governor Cuomo," *The Guardian*, January 24, 2014, https://www.theguardian.com/commentisfree/2014/jan/24/governor-cuomo-conservatives-not-welcome-new-york.

5. Michael Levin, "Want to get work done? Don't hire a millennial, business owner says," *New York Daily News*, April 11, 2016,

http://www.nydailynews.com/life-style/work-don-hire-millennial-biz-owner-article-1.2596941.

6. Louis Efron, "Why Millennials Don't Want To Work For You," *Forbes*, December 13, 2015, https://www.forbes.com/sites/louisefron/2015/12/13/why-millennials-dont-want-to-work-for-you/#490bddc31bef.

7. Laura Stampler, "6 Quotes That Prove Millennials Are Simply Terrible Employees," *Business Insider*, January 3, 2013, http://www.businessinsider.com/6-quotes-prove-millennials-bad-employees-2013-1.

8. Ibid.

12: SEX IN THE FAMILY

1. Vigen Guroian, "Dorm Brothel," *Christianity Today*, January 21, 2005, http://www.christianitytoday.com/ct/2005/february/13.44.html.

2. Ibid.

3. Hollie McKay, "Transgender MSU student's sex assault claim leads accused to fight back in lawsuit," *Fox News*, 28, 2017, http://www.foxnews.com/us/2017/02/28/transgender-msu-student-s-sex-assault-claim-leads-accused-to-fight-back-in-lawsuit.html.

4. Mary Rice Hasson, "Your Tuition Dollars at Work: How Colleges Promote a Perverse Sexual Ideology," Ethics and Public Policy Center, https://eppc.org/publications/your-tuition-dollars-at-work-how-colleges-promote-a-perverse-sexual-ideology/.

5. "Earlier News," *Inside Higher Ed*, November 3, 2016, https://www.insidehighered.com/news/2016/11/03/cdc-finds-sharp-growth-stds-college-agepopulation,%20https://www.cdc.gov/nchhstp/newsroom/docs/factsheets/std-trends-508.pdf .

6. "HIV Among Youth," Centers for Disease Control and Prevention, https://www.cdc.gov/hiv/group/age/youth/.

7. "Colorado district leads middle school students to sexually depraved material and X-rated pornography. School officials attack & threaten parents who object," *Mass Resistance*, January 12, 2017, http://www.massresistance.org/docs/gen3/17a/CO-middle-school-x-rated/index.html.

8. Jason R. Thomas and Robin S. Högnäs, "The Effect of Parental Divorce on the Health of Adult Children," *Longitudinal and Life Course Studies* 6.3 (2015): 279–302.

9. "Obama's Father's Day Remarks," Transcript, *The New York Times*, June 15, 2008, http://www.nytimes.com/2008/06/15/us/politics/15text-obama.html.

10. Mary Parke, "Are Married Parents Really Better for Children?" Center for Law and Social Policy, May 2003, http://www.clasp.org/resources-and-publications/states/0086.pdf.

11. Gretchen Livingston, "Fewer than half of U.S. kids today live in a 'traditional' family," Pew Research Center, December 22, 2014, http://www.pewresearch.org/fact-tank/2014/12/22/less-than-half-of-u-s-kids-today-live-in-a-traditional-family/.

12. Alveda King, "The American Dream Is Deeply Rooted in the Natural Family," Dr. Alveda King's Blog, Priests for Life, http://www.priestsforlife.org/africanamerican/blog/index.php/the-american-dream-is-deeply-rooted-in-the-natural-family.

13. Joseph Price, Robert I. Lerman, and W. Bradford Wilcox, *Strong families, prosperous states: Do healthy families affect the wealth of states?* American Enterprise Institute, October 19, 2015, http://www.aei.org/publication/strong-families-prosperous-states/.

14. Eric Cochling, "Reinvigorating Family Life: Critical to Restoring Opportunity," Medium.com, July 11, 2016, https://medium.com/2016-index-of-culture-and-opportunity/reinvigorating-family-life-critical-to-restoring-opportunity-574ad9bd8adf.

15. Jason Richwine and Robert Rector, "The Fiscal Cost of Unlawful Immigrants and Amnesty to the U.S. Taxpayer," The Heritage Foundation, May 6, 2013, http://www.heritage.org/immigration/report/the-fiscal-cost-unlawful-immigrants-and-amnesty-the-us-taxpayer.

16. Stephen C Goss, "The Future Financial Status of the Social Security Program," *Social Security Bulletin* 70 no. 3 (August 2010), https://www.ssa.gov/policy/docs/ssb/v70n3/v70n3p111.html.

17. Gary S. Becker, *Human Capital: A Theoretical and Empirical Analysis, with Special Reference to Education* (Chicago: University of Chicago Press, 2008).

18. Adam Smith and Andrew S. Skinner, *The Wealth of Nations* (London: Penguin, 1999).

19. Janice Shaw Crouse, "Chicken and egg dilemma about the decline in marriage," *The Washington Times*, May 5, 2015, http://www.washingtontimes.com/news/2015/mar/5/janice-shaw-crouse-chicken-and-egg-dilemma-about-d/#ixzz3TWxlhxAy.

20. Patrick F. Fagan, "Social Capital, the Family and the Economy," World Congress of Families, Madrid, May, 2012; "How the Retreat from Marriage is Hurting the Economy," Love and Fidelity, Network, Princeton, November 2012; Patrick Fagan, Andrew Kidd and Henry Potrykus, *Marriage and Economic Well-Being: The Economy of the Family Rises and Falls with Marriage*, Marriage and Religion Institute, May 4, 2011, http://downloads.frc.org/EF/EF12D58.pdf; Kevin Andrews, *Maybe 'I do': Modern Marriage and the Pursuit of Happiness* (Redland Bay, Australia: Connor Court Publishing, 2012); Allan C. Carlson, *Conjugal America: On the Public Purposes of Marriage* (Piscataway, NJ: Transaction Publishers, 2008).

21. Peter Sprigg,"Homosexual Parent Study: Summary of Findings,"
Family Research Council, http://www.frc.org/issuebrief/
homosexual-parent-study-summary-of-findings.

22. Gertrude Himmelfarb, *One Nation, Two Cultures* (New York:
Alfred A. Knopf, 1999), 28.

13: THANK GOD FOR THE CHURCH

1. David Gibson, "Princeton Theological Seminary reverses decision
to honor Redeemer's Tim Keller," Religion News Service, March
22, 2017, http://religionnews.com/2017/03/22/princeton-
theological-seminary-reverses-decision-to-honor-redeemers-tim-
keller/.

2. Matthew Parris, "As an atheist, I truly believe Africa needs God,"
The Times, December 27, 2008, http://www.thetimes.co.uk/
article/as-an-atheist-i-truly-believe-africa-needs-god-
3xj9bm80h8m.

3. John Blake, "Author: More teens becoming 'fake' Christians,"
CNN, August 27, 2010, http://www.cnn.com/2010/
LIVING/08/27/almost.christian/.

4. Colson and Pearcey, *How Now Shall We Live?*

5. John Wesley, *Essential Works of John Wesley: Selected Books,
Sermons, and Other Writings*, Alice Russie ed. (Uhrichsville, OH:
Barbour Pub Inc., 2013).

6. "The Sermons of John Wesley—Sermon 16—The Means of
Grace," Wesley Center Online, http://wesley.nnu.edu/john-wesley/
the-sermons-of-john-wesley-1872-edition/sermon-16-the-means-
of-grace/.

7. "Groundbreaking ACFI Survey Reveals How Many Adults Have
a Biblical View," American Culture & Faith Institute, February
27, 2017, https://www.culturefaith.com/groundbreaking-survey-

by-acfi-reveals-how-many-american-adults-have-a-biblical-worldview/.

8. Matt Walsh, "Dear Christians, it's not the church's job to make us feel comfortable," *The Blaze*, December 7, 2016, http://www.theblaze.com/contributions/dear-christians-its-not-the-churchs-job-to-make-us-feel-comfortable/.

14: ADVICE FOR CONCERNED PARENTS

1. Sam Abrams, "Professors moved left since 1990s, rest of country did not," Heteredox Academy, January 9, 2016, http://heterodoxacademy.org/2016/01/09/professors-moved-left-but-country-did-not/.

2. David French, *A Season for Justice: Defending the Rights of the Christian Home, Church, and School* (Nashville: Broadmanar and Holman Publishers, 2002).

3. Richard Rorty, "Universality and Truth," 22.

4. Ed Stetzer,"Dropouts and Disciples: How many students are really leaving the church?" *Christianity Today*, May 14, 2014, http://www.christianitytoday.com/edstetzer/2014/may/dropouts-and-disciples-how-many-students-are-really-leaving.html.

5. Michael Lipka, "Why America's 'nones' left religion behind," Pew Research Center, August 24, 2016, http://www.pewresearch.org/fact-tank/2016/08/24/why-americas-nones-left-religion-behind/.

6. Eliot, *"The Aims of Education."*

7. Charles Colson, "The Utopian Impulse," *BreakPoint Commentaries*, September 15, 1999, http://www.thepointradio.org/bpcommentaries/entry/13/13183.

15: THE UNIVERSITY LEADERSHIP VACUUM

1. Ryan Wolfe, "Outnumbered: Conservative Faculty Speak Out," *The Wake Forest Review*, May 1, 2017, http://wakeforestreview. com/outnumbered-conservative-faculty-speak-out/.

2. John Piper, *Desiring God* (Sisters, OR.: Multinomah , 1996).

CONCLUSION: THE UNITY OF FIRST THINGS

1. C. S. Lewis, "First and Second Things," in *God in the Dock: Essays on Theology and Ethics*, Walter Hooper ed. (Grand Rapids: Eerdmans, 1970), 280.

2. R. H. Bork, *Slouching Towards Gomorrah: Modern Liberalism and American Decline* (New York: HarperCollins, 1996), 336.

3. Mark Galli, "The Most Astonishing Easter Miracle," *Christianity Today*, March 17, 2017, http://www.christianitytoday.com/ ct/2017/april/most-astonishing-easter-miracle.html.

INDEX